Let's Get Moving

A Bible Commentary for Laymen/Ephesians
By D. STUART BRISCOE

Regal Books A Division of G/L Publications
Ventura, California, U.S.A.

Other good reading in the Bible Commentary for Laymen series:

Bound for Joy, Commentary on Philippians,
      by D. Stuart Briscoe
Loved and Forgiven, Commentary on Colossians
      by Lloyd John Ogilvie
Liberated for Life, Commentary on Galatians
      by John F. MacArthur

The foreign language publishing of all Regal books is under the direction of GLINT. GLINT provides financial and technical help for the adaptation, translation and publishing of books in more than 85 languages for millions of people worldwide.

For more information write: GLINT, P.O. Box 6688, Ventura, CA 93006.

Scripture quotations, unless otherwise indicated, are from the *Authorized King James Version.*
Others are:
(RSV) from *Revised Standard Version,* copyrighted 1946 and 1952 by the Division of Christian Education of the NCCC, U.S.A., and used by permission.

Fifth Printing, 1980

Published by Regal Books
A Division of G/L Publications
Ventura, California 93006
Printed in U.S.A.

Library of Congress Catalog Card No. 77-91773
ISBN 0-8307-0538-4

Contents

A Teacher's Manual and Student Discovery Guide for
use with *Let's Get Moving* are available from
your church supplier.

Preface

, I preached my first sermon at the ripe old age of 17. It was entitled "The Church at Ephesus." I didn't choose the topic—in fact, I didn't choose to preach at all! I was "volunteered" for both! But two things were born that day. First, a desire to preach God's Word and, second, a great love for the Epistle to the Ephesians. My love for both has grown over the intervening years.

As a young believer I was tremendously helped by studying the passages in the Epistle which deal with the Christian's walk in the power of the living Christ. In fact, the discovery that God is able to do "exceedingly abundantly above all" that I can ask or think according to the power that works in me, was and is totally thrilling to me.

As a husband and father the practical passages relating to interpersonal relationships became a statement of principle upon which my family life has been built. And while the building has sometimes shaken, the foundations have never moved.

As an itinerant preacher I learned that God's people, worldwide, love to be led into the study of life in the "heavenly places." And over the years I have seen not a few people born of the Spirit through an exposition of that most fundamental of statements, "for by grace are ye saved through faith."

As a pastor of a growing church and a minister to pastors, I have constantly referred to Paul's treatment of the Christian ministry with particular reference to the place of the pastor/teacher in "perfecting ... the saints, for the work of the ministry for the edifying of the body of Christ."

And as a disciple of the Lord Jesus for 40 years, I never cease to be overwhelmed when I read again of "the purpose of him who worketh all things after the counsel of his own will, that we should be to the praise of his glory."

Then one glorious day I landed at the little Turkish port of Kusadasi, drove the few winding miles to the site of ancient Ephesus and spent many exciting hours exploring the very places where Paul ministered, survived riots, trained people for the evangelization of Asia Minor and generally let it be known that Jesus Christ is Lord.

In this book I have tried to share with you some of my excitement about Ephesus and the letter written by Paul to the Ephesian believers and, in all probability, those in neighboring towns. I hope that you will find much in the study of this Epistle to enrich your life as it has enriched mine.

1

Let's
Get
Excited!

Ephesians 1:1-12

Recently at the conclusion of a roll-out-the-pulpit, lock-up-the-organ youth presentation, the congregation burst spontaneously into prolonged applause. The leader of the group thanked the people for their obvious appreciation then added, "We really want to direct your attention to the Lord Jesus of whom we have been speaking and singing; so let's express appreciation to Him." Some people would call that corny and others might scream "sacrilege" but the congregation exploded into a sustained expression of thunderous acclaim.

I think Paul the apostle would have understood and he may even have joined in because he got thoroughly excited about the Lord. He barely got through the introduction of his letter to the church in Ephesus before he burst out with an exhilarating expression of appreciation to the Lord: "Blessed be the God and Father of our Lord Jesus Christ" (1:3). In fact, his enthusiasm was so unbounded that his opening sentence went on and on rather like the applause that wouldn't quit! Some Bible commentators have said that Paul's opening expressions of praise defy analysis but none deny that the apostle was thrilled about his Lord!

Blessed Be God

The word "blessed" sets the tone of Paul's appreciation. It is the translation of the Greek word *eulogetos* which means literally, "to speak well of." Paul was speaking well of God because he had learned to think highly of Him. Notice the order of learning—thinking highly and then speaking well of. Sometimes we praise a lot without thinking much because we can't be bothered to learn of Him. Or conversely, we may have learned much theory concerning the Lord but have lost all sense of exhilarating praise.

What was the truth that had so gripped Paul's imagination that it gushed from his lips and spilled from his pen? He had been captivated with the understanding that the God and Father of our Lord Jesus "hath blessed us with all spiritual blessings in heavenly places in Christ." This was no enthusiastic reflex response to an emotional stimulus, but the product of a profound understanding of God Himself with particular reference to His dealings with mankind through the Lord Jesus. He was enthused because he was enlightened.

It was the "blessing" with which God had "blessed" that stimulated Paul to exclaim "blessed." Here we see a broad use of the term "to bless." In effect, Paul said that God thinks so highly of the race

He created that He spoke well of them so as to command that certain things be done for them—thus blessing them. It is a glorious thing to believe that the Father of our Lord Jesus has spoken on our behalf.

Behind the Scenes

There is much more to learn about the ways in which God has worked, particularly as Paul explained the why of God's actions in blessing the human race. He takes us behind the scenes in order that we might see all that has gone into the things that we enjoy. It's rather like watching the young people put on their performance with the added benefit of having been with them through the countless hours of rehearsal and preparation. Those who know the effort that went into the production will be much more enthused than those who only see the end product. Let's follow Paul as he takes us behind the scenes to give us a privileged look at the factors involved in the workings of God.

God showed us His will. Simply stated, God has a plan and a major part of this plan includes the blessing of mankind. Paul said that God acted "according to the good pleasure of his will" (v. 5). Then he added that this plan is not hidden in the recesses of eternity or lost in the unfathomable reaches of the mind of God. On the contrary, God has "made known unto us the mystery of his will" (v. 9).

When Paul talked about the will of God being a mystery he was not suggesting that God, like Agatha Christie, spins incredibly complex tales so that we can exercise our spiritual sleuthing skills in an effort to figure out what on earth He's doing. The word "mystery" means "to reveal what God has kept secret until now"; He is ready to tell us what He is doing.

In addition, Paul taught that the plan was not a heavenly blueprint but an operative event, because the Father is the moving force in its operation. Paul described the Lord as the one "who worketh all things after the counsel of his own will" (v. 11). Our world is not, as some would have us believe, a random collection of colliding molecules populated by millions of animated accidents helplessly assisting cruel fate. Our world is the arena in which God is working out the plan that He devised to bring untold blessing to bear upon us.

Of course, the colossal cosmic aspect of God's activity has had an overwhelming effect on some individuals. Instead of being elated beyond measure, they have become discouraged because of their own apparent insignificance in a scenario of such immense proportions. But this should not be, because even though God's plan is vast it is eminently personal. Paul stated firmly that he was an apostle "by the will of God" (v. 1). So while there is no doubt about the immensity, there should also be no doubt about the intimacy of the divine plan. There is little wonder, therefore, that Paul should be so exhilarated.

God showed us His glory. There is no doubt that our world is deeply in need. While opinions vary greatly concerning the causes and remedies of this need, there is a firm consensus of opinion that something is desperately needed. Christians are firm in their conviction that this something is the blessing of God.

This belief, which is perfectly accurate, has unfortunately led some to think that it was human need that prompted God to bless us, in the same way that an earthquake stimulates nations to send relief or the cry of a drowning man spurs sunbathers into action. However, Paul taught that the blessing of God was part of the plan of God and this plan predated human need because it predated human existence. In fact, the plan to bless originated "before the foundation of the world" (v. 4).

God is concerned about human need, but His intentions to act in the area of human need were crystallized long before the need was there. If you find this hard to grasp, hold on to your seat because Paul also told the Ephesians that God blessed man to bring glory to Himself! God's action is "to the praise of his glory," an expression which Paul repeated three times with slight variations in verses 6,12 and 14.

This thought has been decidedly disquieting to some and downright objectionable to others. Even believers! It must be granted that, at first sight, God does appear to be rather egotistical and more wrapped up in glorifying Himself than in helping poor people in their pain and anguish.

Ray Stedman, in his book, *Riches in Christ*, suggests that many believers think that they must praise God "because His ego needs to be massaged" and that "He will get mad at us and not run things right" unless we praise Him. So they feel they "have to butter Him up a bit to get Him to work."[1] In answer to these misgivings, it should be pointed out that most people are prepared to give credit where it's due and are extremely reluctant to give it if they think it is not due. The main question we should ask is, "Does God deserve any credit or praise?"

We are all duly impressed with award winning athletes who say, "Thank you for this honor but I could never have earned it without the help and support of my teammates." Their humility and modesty are appreciated because everyone realizes the truth of what they are saying. But God has no supporting cast. He needs no teammates to help Him fulfill His purposes. Everything we have and do is a product of something else and needs other things for its survival and function. But God has no one else. He is totally self-supporting and self-sufficient in Himself. There is a sense in which He uses mankind's special qualities to work out His purposes, but God gave man these qualities and we have this unique role only because God purposed to give it to us.

So we can see there is nothing that smacks of pride in God. There is no need for modesty or humility in Him for the simple reason that He is not the greatest, He is the *Only*. Therefore, to praise His glory is to do nothing more than to take a giant stride toward reality and away from the fantasy world where man is greater than God and where the solution of earthly problems is more important than the unfolding of the eternal plan of the ages. It is to gladly and ungrudgingly give God credit for being God.

God showed us His grace. Behind God's "blessing" activity there is another factor that delights the believer's heart—the grace of God. Paul used words like "riches" and "glory" to describe the grace of God. I find it helpful to think of grace in its relationship to justice and mercy.

Justice administers what I deserve.
Mercy delivers me from all that I deserve.
Grace bestows upon me what I will never
deserve.

Justice is a stern judge sitting on his bench, administering the law. Mercy is that same judge feeling the pain of the guilty one, understanding his problems, recognizing extenuating circumstances and giving the lightest possible punishment. But grace is the judge removing his robes of office, standing with the guilty party, taking out his checkbook, paying the fine, leading him out of court to his own home and making him a member of his own family with all the rights and privileges of family membership. We call these rights and privileges "all spiritual blessings in [the heavenlies] in Christ" (1:3).

Many people who recognize their sinfulness would be glad if God would offer them mercy. But they don't understand that mercy without grace is not only inadequate to meet the human need, it is also a totally inadequate expression of God's character. Like the returned prodigal they would be grateful if they could get a little corner in the servants' quarters. But God, like the prodigal's father, won't hear of it. "Bring forth the best robe and put it on him, a ring on his finger and shoes on his feet and bring out the food and let's have a feast of celebration for this is my son back where he belongs in my family" (see Luke 15:22,23). That is the riches of the glory of His grace towards us. And remember that this demonstration of grace is really a projection of the reality of God's person and a revelation of who He really is.

God showed us His love. The phrase "in love"

(Eph. 1:4) has caused some minor headaches for Bible students because in the Greek it can relate to either the preceding or succeeding phrases. So it could mean He has chosen us in love or we "should be holy and without blame before him in love." Both are true and so, while we cannot be dogmatic about Paul's exact meaning, we can apply the phrase as a further expression of God's motivation behind the blessing He has made available.

Love is something of which we talk regularly and about which we sing fervently. But love is love only when it gets around to acting. Love is much more than a warm feeling or golden glow. It is a determined action that may or may not be accompanied with positive feelings. Loving is different from liking. You may like without loving and love without liking, although doing both is bliss! God didn't like the world. If He had liked it, He would presumably have left it in a rotten mess. But God *loved* the world. And because He loved what He disliked, He acted to put things right. He shows the reality of His love in His saving and "blessing" activities.

Spiritual Blessings

One of the problems about the word "blessing" is that it is used so loosely. But Paul was very specific when he talked about the blessing of God. He said it was "spiritual." This means that while he was thoroughly practical in his approach to life in general and Christian living in particular, he knew that the essence of the working of God in people's lives is spiritual. This is an important thought because our contemporary world gets excited about physical, tangible realities but often gives scant attention to the spiritual aspects of life, which Scripture teaches is far more important.

Then Paul added that the blessings were to be found "in heavenly places" or more accurately "in the heavenlies." This was a favorite Pauline expression. He taught that there was a realm of experience quite distinct from the world, which our society calls the "real world." In the same way that our atmosphere is full of sound waves of which we are totally unaware until we tune in our radios, so the natural world is permeated with the unseen, unknown world of the heavenlies. Many people know nothing of this world of spiritual delight and blessing and never will unless they are tuned into the wave length of the heavenlies.

This tuning process takes place, as Paul points out, when we are "in Christ." This is probably the most common expression in the Ephesians letter. In the first few verses of the letter it is very clear that the sphere of spiritual blessing known as the heavenlies is only available to those who have a relationship known as being in Christ. For a fuller treatment of this beautiful truth, which I like to call the province of spiritual experience, you may like to refer to my book *The Fullness of Christ*.[2]

Once we are clear about these facts concerning the blessing of God and the stupendous divine motivation behind His intervention in the human area, we can safely explore the details of the blessing available. For the sake of making it easy to remember the details, I am going to present them to you in alphabetical order.

A—in Christ God adopts us. I once had to minister to a family having some problems with one of their teenagers. Rightly or wrongly, they had not told the young person that he was an adopted child and he had found out through the gossip of some of his classmates. Quite understandably, he was greatly disturbed and reacted quite strongly. But one day he told me that he had stopped resenting his adoption when he realized that he was a member of the family for no other reason than his parents really wanted him and that was something a natural born child could not be so sure about! He was wanted!

Part of the foreordained plan was that God would bring people into His family despite the fact that they had forfeited this place through their sin. They would have full status as sons including being "an heir of God through Christ" (Gal. 4:7). So if you are in Christ, you are a child of God through adoption and you should be excited about that if only because it means you're wanted by God!

B—in Christ God blesses us. At the risk of laboring the point, I want to add one vital thing to what we have already seen about "all spiritual blessing." The word "blessing" is in the singular and the tense of "has blessed" is the aorist, so Paul literally said God has blessed us, in Christ, with a totality of spiritual blessing. It is an accomplished fact and it is to be regarded as thoroughly complete. This is tremendously exciting because it means that once in Christ we don't have to wonder if we are going to lack anything. We have all blessing in Christ. Neither do we have to wonder where to look for the blessing. It is all in Christ. It's rather like going into a store at the

16

beach where they have absolutely everything you need for fishing and camping and sailing. There's no need to go anywhere else!

C—in Christ God chooses us. It is obvious that God did some deciding before anything happened because if He hadn't, nothing would have happened! But what did He decide?

Among other things, God decided that all those who are in Christ should live before Him holy and without blemishes. This refers not only to our eternal destiny, but also to the life-style He chose we should adopt before we get as far as eternity. We should note particularly that "to choose" means literally "to call out." This reminds us that God has chosen to call people to Himself so that they can be holy before Him and also that this call requires the response of man in obedience and faith. Extreme positions have been taken in the whole area of "election" and "free will" but it should be clear that anything that denies God's right to take initiatives or denies man's respon- sibility to respond is an unbalanced position. Richard Halverson, in his masterly way, said, "Nothing God planned interferes with human freedom . . . . Nothing humans do frustrates God's sovereign plan!"[3]

D—in Christ God delivers us. "Redemption through his blood" (v. 7) is part of the blessing in Christ. Most people only use the word redemption in today's society on the rare occasions when they deal with stocks or mortgages. But in Paul's day the word *apolutrosis* meant literally "to loose from" and was used to describe "prisoners of war, slaves and crimi- nals condemned to death," according to F. Buchsel in the *Theological Dictionary of the New Testament.*[4]

17

The idea conveyed by the word is that of ransom being paid to deliver those incapable of freeing themselves. This is part of the blessing of God through Christ; His blood (which means His life surrendered) being the price of the ransom paid.

E—in Christ God enriches us. "In whom also we have obtained an inheritance" (v. 11) suggests that we have been enriched by God to the point of receiving vast resources from Him. But the expression in the Greek probably refers more to the idea that we have become His inheritance. In the same way that Moses sang, "For the Lord's portion is his people" (Deut. 32:9), so those in Christ have become the special possession of the Lord, dear to His heart. In this way they have both "become" and "received" an inheritance, and both ways are immeasurably blessed.

F—in Christ God forgives us. We have already seen something of the "riches of his grace" but, at this point, we need to reflect on one of the Lord's actions which shows His grace in a special way. It is in the "forgiveness of sins" (v. 7). The Greek word is *aphesis* which is translated "remission" more often than "forgiveness" in the New Testament.

The Lord told the story of a man deeply, hopelessly in debt who, when he expressed his inability to pay, was told to sell his wife and children into slavery to raise the necessary funds. Understandably, this was more than the poor man could take, so he fell pleading before his creditor who was so moved by the man's plight that he "loosed him, and forgave him the debt" (Matt. 18:27). God has been moved with compassion toward us and has removed from us an obli-

18

gation to pay for our trespasses. This is forgiveness.

G—*in Christ God gathers us.* We might ask ourselves, Where is all this mighty work of God going to end? The answer is in "the fulness of times" (v. 10). God will bring everything to a climax when He gathers "all things" to Himself. In complete contrast to the existing state of fragmentation and disintegration which we see on every hand, there will be a oneness in Christ. Things will fit, everything will make sense to such a degree that the God whose command brought all things into being and whose blessing restored the ravaged remains of His broken masterpiece will be shown to be the gracious, glorious, superlative God that He is. Order will prevail where chaos reigned. Holiness will shine where darkness brooded and all the shoddy, shabby plans of man will lie shattered under the completed purposes of the eternal Lord. And right there in the middle of it all will be you—assuming, of course, that you are in Christ!

Notes

1. Ray Stedman, *Riches in Christ* (Waco, Texas: Word Books, 1976), p. 15.
2. D. Stuart Briscoe, *The Fullness of Christ* (Grand Rapids: Zondervan Publishing House, 1965), p. 65.
3. Richard Halverson, *Perspective* (Grand Rapids: Zondervan Publishing House, 1970).
4. F. Buchsel, *Theological Dictionary of the New Testament*, vol. 4, p. 352.

Eye-Opening Christianity

Ephesians 1:13-23

To be "in Christ" is to be in the area of experience where all the blessings which we have been considering in the last chapter become a reality. But we should not assume that we are automatically "in Christ." In fact, Paul, writing to the Corinthians, insisted that some are "in Christ" while some are "in Adam" (1 Cor. 15:22). Therefore, we should see the options available and investigate our position very carefully and take whatever steps may be necessary.

All a person has to do to be in Adam—that is to be identified with all that Adam stands for—is absolutely nothing. Of course, many people take active steps to show their glad association with Adam in his sinful disobedience.

Positioned "in Christ"

To step out of Adam and take a position in Christ, where all the blessings of Christ are reckoned to a person, requires decisive action.

Paul told the Ephesians that they had *trusted* Christ—they had placed their hope and confidence in Him. Prior to doing that, however, they had *heard* the word of truth, the gospel of [their] salvation, and believed what they had heard (1:13).

The three steps are quite clear. First, we must hear the gospel. Then we must believe the gospel. Then we trust the Christ of the gospel.

Hearing the gospel requires more of us than allowing sounds emanating from the throat of a preacher to bombard our eardrums. The Scripture speaks of those who have ears to hear but don't hear. They have technical equipment but the sounds bounce off their eardrums rather than sink into the depths of their consciousness. To hear the word of the gospel is to be struck forcibly with the immensity of the divine revelation to such an extent that the whole person becomes moved by the truth he receives.

Believing the gospel is the next logical step that is necessary after the truth has been heard. This requires intellectual activity to reach a conclusion that the information received is absolutely trustworthy and accurate. Always remember that Christian experience is not a series of feelings but the intelligent response to well authenticated facts. Many people who have been influenced by our contemporary society live almost exclusively in the realm of the feelings. If they feel good they are happy; if they don't feel good they don't go to work; if they lose love feelings they get a divorce. Christian experience, however, is related to facts that may or may not affect feelings, and solid spiritual experience requires that people arrive at definite conclusions which in turn

21

will lead to solid convictions concerning the gospel.

It may come as a surprise to some that the devils have gone so far as to believe and tremble (see Jas. 2:19) but no one would suggest that they are in Christ. The devils have taken the first steps, they hear and believe, but have failed to take the crucial third step.

The third step is trusting the Christ of the gospel. The fundamental fact of the Christian gospel is that Jesus Christ is Saviour and Lord. When this becomes a clear conviction in a person's mind, action becomes necessary. It would be nonsense to insist in a conviction concerning the saving merits of Christ without claiming them and living in the good of them. In the same way, no one can say that Christ is Lord with any degree of conviction and then live a life denying His controlling lordship. Therefore, the great need is for people to trust themselves to His saving work and commit themselves to His lordship. This takes a person finally out of Adam into Christ.

There are those who have listened but not heard, those who have heard but not believed, and those who have believed but not trusted. And they are all outside of Christ. But those who have listened, *heard*, *believed* and *trusted* are "in Him."

Sealed with the Holy Spirit

There is further evidence to this fact that must be deeply appreciated. Those who are "in Christ" are "sealed with that holy Spirit of promise" (v. 13) who is described as the "earnest of our inheritance" (v. 14). In Paul's time, seals were affixed to documents and other important items by the owner to demon-

22

strate their authenticity. Christ sends the Holy Spirit into the lives of those who are in Christ to show they are for real. To the new believer the ministry of the seal is to convince the believer he is really in Christ. The seal ministers to the unbeliever by changing the life of the believer and to watching angelic beings; the seal gives conclusive evidence that the one He indwells is in Christ.

The Holy Spirit is further described as "the earnest of our inheritance." This means, literally, a "down payment." If the Holy Spirit indwelling us is only part payment, just think about all that is around the corner for those who are in Christ! He is our seal and the evidence of God's intentions for us. He will bring us to final full redemption and if we are ever tempted to doubt it then we should remember who the Holy Spirit is, where He is and what He is doing there in His special role to those "in Christ."

Prayer for the Saints

There is a tendency to settle down once the initial excitement of any experience has worn thin. Paul, continually aware of this possibility, tried not only to lead people to Christ but also to lead them into ever-deepening relationships with Him. His prayer for the Ephesians beautifully illustrates his concern and also his understanding of dimensions of spiritual growth that could reasonably be expected of the Ephesians. There was, of course, no doubt that they had come a long way from the days of the riot in the arena and the worship of Diana (see Acts 19:23-41). But while it was undoubtedly good for them to look back once in a while to see where they had *come from*, it was

23

necessary for them to look forward to see where they were *going to!*

It is unlikely that many of us stop in the middle of writing a letter to pray for the one to whom we are writing, but to Paul this was not unusual. When he shared the vast truths which God had revealed to him he was often overcome with a great sense of praise and intercession. This is exactly what happened as he wrote to the Ephesians as the word "wherefore" (v. 15) clearly demonstrates. In the light of all that he had been writing he had to pray. In addition, the news that he had been receiving concerning their spiritual progress was a further stimulus to his prayers.

We usually get around to praying when we receive bad news. Next time you go to a prayer meeting make a note of how many disasters are presented as reasons for prayer. No doubt, someone will mention Mrs. Jones' forthcoming surgery, Mr. Smith's upcoming burial and the impending church meeting. By no means would I wish to suggest that these items do not merit prayer, but it is unfortunate that the impression is conveyed all too often that prayer is something you do when everything goes wrong.

Paul had received only good news from Ephesus and that was why he wanted to pray. He was so grateful for all that was going on that he wanted to ensure, through prayer, that the momentum was maintained and the progress continued.

Uppermost in the apostle's mind was that he had heard of their "faith in the Lord Jesus, and love unto all the saints" (v. 15). When people talked about the church at Ephesus, the topics were faith and love. I think if we came across a church where people were talking about the faith that was visible and the love that was tangible we might be tempted to think that that particular church didn't need prayer and turn our attention to a more "normal" situation! But I think Paul is reminding us that the most effective church is the most vulnerable and the most dedicated church is the most likely to succeed and on both counts needs much prayer.

Understandably his prayer started with thanksgiving which is where prayer ought to start. When prayer becomes a shopping list and God a cut-rate supermarket operator, something big has disappeared from our relationship with Him. But if we are careful to come into His presence with praise and stand before Him in thanksgiving, the focus is more on His majesty than our poverty and His glory than our selfishness. This produces an atmosphere where real communion—which, after all, is the essence of prayer —can take place. Note also that his praying was an ongoing thing. He made a habit of being in the Lord's presence. He prayed ceaselessly.

Paul's request was simply, "*that the God of our Lord Jesus Christ, the Father of glory,*" *would graciously grant to the believers* "*the spirit of wisdom and revelation*" (v. 17). Did I say simply? When he used the word "spirit" he was probably referring to the human spirit rather than the Holy Spirit. He desired that they should have fresh revelations from the Lord, deep in the areas of their spirit which would lead to increased wisdom.

Those familiar with Paul's first letter to Corinth, in which he roundly castigated the Corinthians for their interest in wisdom, may be surprised to see him not only advocating its necessity but praying for it to be granted to the Ephesians. But we should point out that Paul very clearly differentiated between the philosophical wisdom of the Greeks, which was nothing more than brilliant speculation, and the revelation of eternal truth available to believers through the work of the Holy Spirit in their lives. This, of course, was far superior to anything man could come up with.

This is not to suggest that Paul was anti-intellectual. Rather, he firmly believed that all there is to know of God comes from revelation not speculation. But when revelation has been given and gladly received, then all the intellectual powers should be brought to bear upon the mind-blowing things that God has shown through His Spirit. There is no end to things God has to show us, and no limit to the riches of His purposes on our behalf. So the time will never come, this side of eternity, when a believer needs no further revelations or is excused from further intellectual activity to grapple with the revelations.

When we talk about revelations, of course, we are in tricky territory. We step into the area where all manner of eccentricities and esoteric experiences abound. As our contemporary society is particularly enamored of all manner of purely subjective experiences, the more outlandish the better, there has been a tendency in the church to concentrate on this type of subjectivism and to interpret it as divine revelation. Considerable care is necessary at this point because all manner of chicanery and tomfoolery is being foisted on the church in the name of the Lord under the guise of it being revealed by the Lord.

Paul had nothing of this nature in mind when he prayed for further revelation that would result in added wisdom "in the knowledge of him" (v. 17). It cannot be stated too strongly that Christ is the one "in whom are hid all the treasures of wisdom and knowledge" (Col. 2:3). Therefore, any "revelation" contrary to that which Christ taught or in opposition to all He stands for is not for the believer.

"The knowledge of him" means experiential knowledge rather than academic knowledge. The phrase has in mind the experience of knowing a person rather than knowing about a person. The Bible consistently teaches that spiritual experience is directly related to knowing God through His Son. The writer of Proverbs clearly stated that "the knowledge of the holy" one is the key to understanding (Prov. 9:10). The Lord Jesus insisted that eternal life consists of knowing "the only true God, and Jesus Christ" (John 17:3).

Paul in another place expressed the personal conviction that the "excellency of the knowledge of Christ Jesus my Lord" (Phil. 3:8) was the primary thing in his life. He added that his major objective was to "know him, and the power of his resurrection, and the fellowship of his sufferings" (3:10). This was a desire right in line with Peter's exhortation to "grow . . . in the knowledge of our Lord and Saviour Jesus Christ" (2 Pet. 3:18).

Fuller knowledge of the things of God comes through deeper acquaintance with the living Christ as a reality in our lives. This is achieved in much the same way that we become more deeply acquainted with any other person.

Time, Talk and Trust

In my experience it takes the three t's to grow in the knowledge of a person: time, talk and trust.

Time must be spent with the Lord. This means special times when He is the center of our attention. It also means spending all the time in touch with Him even when we are not aware of Him. My wife and I have discovered that we enjoy time together but we also find great happiness in knowing the other one is around somewhere even if we don't know where. We even find ourselves thinking the same thoughts, having the same convictions and taking the same actions even though we may not be in physical contact. In other words, we spend all our time together even though we sometimes find ourselves on opposite sides of the world.

Herman Nicolas had a hard time as a lay monk working in a monastery kitchen as Brother Lawrence until he recognized that he could serve and know the Lord there as well as any other place. His attitude changed and his life-style with it and from the experience came the classic devotional book, *The Practice of the Presence of God*. This kind of time spent with Him is the pathway to further revelations of Him.

Talking with the Lord is obviously closely related to time spent with Him. In my book *Getting into God*,[1] I defined prayer as "the talking part of a relationship" with God. So when we talk about talking with the Lord, there is obviously the thought of careful attention to prayer in the community of believers and personal devotions, but also the practice of talking to the Lord in the everyday occurrences of life. Driving, walking, running, sitting at a desk, bending over a cradle, sweating at a furnace, or lying in the sun. Just communing silently or audibly with him.

Trusting a person is a great way to get to know him. We have a tendency to insist that people show themselves trustworthy before we will trust them. But this is a little hard on them because the only way they can prove themselves trustworthy is by showing themselves worthy of trust which even the greatest saint cannot do if he is never trusted! Somewhere along the line a step of faith has to be taken.

Right at this time I am working with a young man from a minority race who has suffered misfortune after misfortune—some because of his own stupidity, others because of the harsh prejudiced treatment of others. But nobody knows what he can do because nobody ever went out on a limb and trusted him with some responsibility. So I have done just that and he is slowly showing us some hitherto hidden capabilities. I'm holding my breath, but the more he comes through, the more easily I'm breathing.

Trusting the Lord is the way to find out what He can do. But the one who never trusts Him never discovers Him in fullness and, accordingly, is short on revelation and wisdom.

Spiritual Enlightenment

The man who had his eyesight restored by the Lord Jesus at first saw "men as trees, walking" (Mark 8: 24), but later had fuller vision and clearer understanding. In the same way, Paul's desire for the Ephesians was that their spiritual understanding might be enlightened. He prayed, literally, that the eyes of their hearts might be opened. In Paul's day, the heart was understood to be the whole person rather than the seat of the emotions as we would tend to use the expression. So he was eager that their whole being should be diffused with enlightenment, not just their minds or their emotions.

The prayer becomes very specific at this point as Paul stated the three areas in which the enlightening and the growing should take place. He wanted them to grow in their knowledge of the hope of His calling, the riches of the glory of His inheritance, and the exceeding greatness of His power (see vv. 18,19).

Paul wanted the Ephesians to know "the hope of his calling." We use the word "hope" in widely different ways. When there is no hope we still insist on hoping. But when we are overwhelmingly confident we still talk about hope. The kid who gets straight F's in school hopes to graduate while the kid who gets straight A's also hopes to graduate. They use the same word but will probably not have the same experience.

Sometimes we talk about Christian hope with a tremor in our voices and a tremble on our lips. We should. And we should act as if we hope where there is no hope when, in actual fact, Christian hope is overwhelming confidence.

This hope among other things comes from an understanding of "his calling"—that to which He has called or invited us. The New Testament makes many references to this aspect of our salvation. It refers to our "high calling" (Phil. 3:14), our "holy calling" (2 Tim. 1:9), and our "heavenly calling" (Heb. 3:1). All these terms express the wonder of the fact that the Lord has invited us in the first place and then the unbelievable blessings that are part of the invitation.

To understand that He has invited you because He wants you to participate in all that is involved in a high, heavenly and holy experience is to sense the thrill of being part of something so far beyond yourself that it will need all the power and the grace of God to bring it to fruition. This, in turn, leads to a great sense of confidence that it will really happen because "Faithful is he that calleth you, who also will do it" (1 Thess. 5:24). Self-confident people are tiresome, but Christians who are lacking in confidence are equally tiresome because they exhibit so little understanding of the commitment of God to finalize that which He initiated when He called them to Himself.

Then Paul requested that the Ephesians might know "the riches of the glory of his inheritance in the saints" (v. 18). Earlier Paul mentioned that the Holy Spirit is the earnest of our inheritance, but here he talks about the glorious richness of "his inheritance." Some commentators believe that Paul is referring to the same thing on both occasions even though he uses different terms. But there are others who believe that Paul was carefully differentiating between what is in Christ for us and what is in us for Christ. His inheritance is what God has given Him, our inheritance is what God has given us. God has given Christ to us and God has given us to Christ. Christ is our inheritance, we are His.

To see yourself as Christ's inheritance, God's gift to His well-beloved Son, is mind shattering. Few things are more conducive to disciplined living and

31

loving commitment than the thought that all Christ has on earth from the Father are redeemed individuals. Yet Paul says we are not a poor inheritance but rather gloriously rich. Later in the Epistle we shall see that he refers to us as being Christ's Body, Christ's building and Christ's bride. In this light we can begin to look at ourselves through His eyes and, accordingly, get a clearer vision.

Paul's final request is that the Ephesians might come to realize "what is the exceeding greatness of his power to us-ward who believe, according to the working of his mighty power" (v. 19). Francis Foulkes, in his commentary on *Ephesians*, wrote that Paul in his desire to convey the greatness of the divine power "expresses this in the strongest terms that language can find."[2]

Indeed Paul did use four of the strongest terms to speak of God's power: "power" is *dunamis* from which we derive "dynamic"; "working" is *energeia* which needs no explanation; "mighty" is *kratos* which has found its way into English in such words as autocratic, democratic; and another word for "power," *ischus*. All this adds up to a mighty statement of the operation of God "to us-ward who believe."

Not satisfied that he had made himself clear enough, Paul thought of an illustration that would put it all beyond any doubt. He talked about the greatest of all demonstrations of power seen in the action of God in raising Christ from the dead, raising Him to His own right hand and seating Him there in total control of all powers and authorities of this age and in the age to come (see v. 20).

Not only that, but in case there was any doubt about the immensity of God's power, Paul finalized it all by insisting that God had "put all things under his feet" (v. 22). That accounts for everything this side of the grave and on the other side, too.

What eye-opening things there are in store for those who deepen in their knowledge of Christ!

Notes

1. D. Stuart Briscoe, *Getting into God* (Grand Rapids: Zondervan Publishing House, 1975), p. 43.
2. Francis Foulkes, *The Epistle of Paul to the Ephesians* Tyndale Bible Commentary (London: Tyndale Press; Grand Rapids: Wm. B. Eerdman's Publishing Co., 1963), p. 62.

3

A Lot To Be Humble About

Ephesians 2:1-10

Winston Churchill had little admiration for his political rival, Clement Atlee, and rarely had anything good to say about him. One day his friends were surprised, therefore, when he reputedly volunteered the information, "Clement Atlee is a very humble man." After a suitable pause he added with a Churchillian twinkle, "Of course, he has a lot to be humble about!"

It is not hard for human beings to adopt a humble attitude when we are conversant with the biblical teaching on the human condition and the divine remedy, because we have much to be humble about! There is no doubt that God expects this attitude. In fact, He reserves some of His strongest words for those who refuse to humble themselves. Paul not only found it possible to turn from his arrogant pharisaical attitudes but also took great delight in the way he had been humbled before God. He was even excited about being humble!

What We Demonstrated

Paul told the Ephesians and he tells us that we should be excited about being humble because there is nothing to boast about in what we demonstrate.

We demonstrated that we were dead. According to Paul's startling announcement the Ephesians "were dead in trespasses and sins" (v. 1). When the Ephesians received the letter announcing this remarkable news, they were not tempted to think that Paul was trying to persuade them that they had suffered a churchwide epidemic to which they had all succumbed after which they had been "quickeneth together" (v. 5). They knew he was not referring to physical deadness but something more serious—spiritual deadness.

When Paul wrote to Timothy he said, "She that liveth in pleasure is dead while she liveth" (1 Tim. 5:6). So there is no doubt that he believed in the strange possibility of life and deadness coexisting in one person. If we accept the fact that we are spiritual as well as physical, it is not difficult to see that a person can be physically alive while spiritually dead, or even spiritually alive while physically dead.

To be physically alive is to be alert to the physical environment and to be spiritually alive means to be aware of the spiritual. Paul was telling the Ephesians that while they were very much alive to their goddess Diana, the games in the stadium, and the financial concerns they had when the trade for the silver statues of Diana began to decline, they had no interest in the Lord, no consciousness of His importance, no relationship with Him whatsoever. They were dead to God, while very much alive to Ephesus. It is easy to see the resemblance of a similar condition today.

We demonstrated we were deluded. Behavior is the result of many factors, but among the most influential are peer pressure and community standards. We are all inveterate conformists. Even those of us who pride ourselves in nonconformity often find it necessary to conform to the standards of other nonconformists. What people say about us and think about us can carry enormous weight in the decision-making process. The importance of this factor in our life-styles is determined by the kind of pressure to which we are being subjected and the nature of the standards to which we are conforming. The fact that "everybody is doing it" may be good or bad depending on what they are doing!

Paul said that human beings operate basically "according to the course of this world" (v. 2). By this he meant that there is a certain attitude or spirit abroad in our present age that discounts the age to come and has little interest in the standards of that era. So when it comes down to it, most people are governed more by contemporary standards than eternal truth and feel more pressured by what people think than by what God has said.

The attitudes and philosophies of this world were exposed brilliantly by John in his first Epistle when he not only showed their roots but also clearly demonstrated their fruits (1 John 2:16). He classified the roots of contemporary behavior as "the lust of the flesh, and the lust of the eyes, and the pride of life." That means we are governed by the contemporary attitudes which insist that the important things are that "my passions" be given free course, "my possessions" are my own business and "my position" is that which no one else must challenge.

So we are producing people by the thousands who live for their passions, their possessions and their own position, which, in a word, is *selfishness*. John said all this was "not of the Father" and added that it would all pass away (1 John 2:16,17). Therefore, all those who live for the contemporary and indulge in the popular philosophies of existence will one day discover that all they lived for has vanished into the broad blue yonder and they are left clutching a hollow dream in one hand and an empty delusion in the other.

We demonstrated that we were dominated. In addition to demonstrating that we, like the Ephesians, are dead and deluded, Paul said that we are also governed by "the prince of the power of the air, the spirit that now worketh in the children of disobedience" (v. 2). Scholars have a little problem with the grammar at this point, but they have no difficulty seeing here a reference to the activity of evil powers in the world as a whole and in individuals specifically.

The word "worketh" used here is related to the word explained in the previous chapter where Paul referred to the powerful activity of God in raising Christ from the dead (see Eph. 1:19,20). But here the reference is clearly to the energetic activity the opponent of God exerts in the hearts of men and women. This power emanating from the devil himself is so strong that human beings find themselves dominated by it to such a degree that they may even do, in their better moments, what they hate and fail to do and in their nobler moments, what they committed themselves to do. This is the awfulness of the inner domination of the fallen race of mankind.

We demonstrated we were disobedient. The result of being surrounded by a society that is at best ignoring God and at worst actively opposing Him, and being dominated by an inner force originating with the one who is flatly opposed to all the purposes of God, is a life of disobedience. The struggle needed to combat the external forces of the "world" and the inner forces of the "prince" has consistently proved too much for the world's population. So we have produced life-styles of disobedience to our God.

Disobedience falls into two categories. First, we have failed to do what God required and, second, we have insisted on doing what God forbade. There is no person who would stand to his feet and deny this statement. So we can see that on the basis of what we as a race have demonstrated, we have much to be humble about.

What We Did

Next we need to see what has transpired because of the things that have been demonstrated. We need to be aware of the things we have done.

We have enjoyed many deviations as Paul clearly showed by his use of the word "trespasses" (v. 1). When I was a small boy I once saw a sign which said, "Trespassers will be prosecuted." I asked my dad what the sign meant but his answer was more striking than accurate. He said, "That means if you climb that fence you will be propped up and shooted." To trespass does mean to climb over a fence or cross over a line, but "prosecute" does not mean you will be propped up and shooted! "Trespass" is the action that takes place when disobedient people cross the limit or step over the boundaries of God's revealed parameters of human behavior. Humanity has deviated from this standard through the years and we continue to do so on every hand.

Paul in the first chapter of his letter to the Romans went further and said bluntly that those who trespass not only get a great charge out of deviant behavior but take great delight in encouraging others to do the same thing (see Rom. 1:32). A clear indictment of what passes for normal behavior in today's world.

We have encountered many defeats as a result of all that has transpired in our lives. To understand what Paul means by "sins" (v. 1) we need to realize that the word he used was commonly used by the Greeks to mean "not to hit," or "to miss," with particular reference to aiming at a target and missing it completely. This is defeat—a failure. Many people feel that when they sin, they are demonstrating their maturity and evidencing their liberty. But actually, they are projecting their failure and portraying their defeat. Instead of showing their world what success they have made out of their struggle to escape from the restrictions of divine principle, they are letting their world know the enormity of their inability to be the people they were created to be.

We have encouraged many desires as we have lived "in the lusts of our flesh, fulfilling the desires of the flesh" (v. 3). Lust tends to have a bad connotation in our contemporary usage but originally it referred to any kind of desire, whether good or bad. However, there is no doubt that Paul, when he talked about the lusts of the flesh, was referring to the desires welling up in the hearts of people living independently of God or in blatant opposition to Him.

Human beings have clearly demonstrated through their long history that they are capable of anything if they desire something! "No holds barred" is the motto in many fields of endeavor in the human arena unless, of course, other factors which might control man's natural desires are brought into the reckoning. Moral restraint, ethical principle and spiritual principle are the only things that can be voluntarily introduced into man's thinking to harness his desires. But if these things are lacking, anything can happen, and usually does as most people can readily testify.

We entertained many designs. Many of man's unsavory and unsatisfactory actions come not only from unbridled desire but also from carefully calculated design. As Paul said, we have succumbed not only to the "flesh" but also to the "mind" (v. 3).

Many of us can look back to specific times in our lives when we were confronted with a situation that required a decision. The options relating to the decision were clearly understood and the consequences of the options were equally clear. We knew the difference between right and wrong, and were fully acquainted with the things that "wrong" would produce and the results that "right" would bring forth. We carefully evaluated the attractiveness of "wrong" as opposed to the burden and discipline of "right." Then we gambled on the consequences and chose wrong with our eyes wide open. This was not sin in the heat of a moment or a mistake in the confusion of a complex issue, but a cold, calculating choice to go against

God. We may feel there are some extenuating circumstances if we fall because unbearable pressure hits us on the blind side. But there is no excuse, whatsoever, for this kind of sin and it is extremely humbling to be reminded of our actions in this respect.

What We Deserved

As a result of the behavior outlined above we are called "children of wrath." This, of course, refers to God's wrath. Sometimes it is difficult for people to accept the fact that a God of love is also described as a God of wrath. As the concept of love is much more attractive than the concept of wrath, there has been a dangerous tendency in contemporary circles to discount the statements about God's wrath and concentrate on the love aspects. This is not only an unwarranted approach to Scripture but also an evidence of inadequate thought processes.

The love of God is shown in His anger against that which destroys and ruins those whom He loves. Loving, gentle mothers often show the intensity of their love for their children by the ferocity with which they defend them and vehemence with which they attack that which threatens their offspring. In this instance, the fierceness is just as much an evidence of love as the gentleness. The only difference being that the gentleness promotes the object of love, while the fierceness is directed at the opponent of the object of love. God loves sinners to distraction and hates sin to the same degree. Strange as it may seem, His love can be discerned in His wrath.

A further point that should be borne in mind is that

when we think of wrath or anger, we think of man's wrath which is so often tainted with unseemly selfishness and unpleasant behavior. But God's wrath is as pure as His love and as holy as His righteousness. When God acts in wrath, He acts in a manner that is totally consistent with His person and thoroughly compatible with His nature. He is perfectly angry!

Once we stop fighting the biblical statements concerning the wrath of God and see the utter consistency of it and the awful purity of it, there will be no trouble accepting the justice of it. In the light of all we have considered so far, there is no doubt that we have deserved it!

What God Displayed

But now it is time to look at the brighter side of the picture as we consider the action of God in the area of human need and deprivation.

Four beautiful words are used by Paul to express the magnificent display of God's nature in His attitude toward those whom He had made and who rebelled against Him—*mercy, love, grace, kindness.* Glorious as these words are, they are not adequate to express Paul's feeling about God's activity in the behalf of humanity, so he elaborated on them.

"But God who is rich in mercy . . . " (v. 4). W.E. Vine, in his *Expository Dictionary of New Testament Words,* defined *mercy* as "the outward manifestation of pity; it assumes need on the part of him who receives it, and resources adequate to meet the need on the part of him who shows it."[1] To that we can add: We need mercy greatly and God has resources to dispense it richly.

"Great love wherewith, he loved us . . . " (v. 4). The *love* of God has as its hallmark the distinct fact that it stems from the being of God rather than being stimulated by the beauty of man. That God loves mankind is due not to man being so irresistibly lovely, lovable and loving but because it is in the nature of God to love whether the object of His love is lovely or not.

The whole story of God's love toward us in Christ Jesus is one of determined love that persisted without much encouragement. In fact, the love of God triumphed over rank opposition, the high point being reached on a cross outside the walls of Jerusalem. There a loving God made Christ to be sin for our race at the very moment when some of the race were showing their hostility through hurling epithets at the suffering Servant and gambling for His discarded clothing. But Love's response to this was, "Father, forgive them; for they know not what they do" (Luke 23:34)!

There are few things I find more humbling than to realize that God's love for me continues when I am at my most unloving and undeserving.

"The exceeding riches of his grace, in his kindness toward us . . . " (v. 7). There is a tendency in our world to be so taken up with human rights that we fail to realize that there is a limit to our rights. A good case can be made for human beings having "unalienable rights" such as "life, liberty, and the pursuit of happiness." "A fair day's pay for a fair day's work" also meets with the approval of most people.

But where do human rights end? Can we say to God, "I have the right to go to heaven"? Or is there a man alive who can approach God and demand eternal life as his unalienable right? The Scriptures make it uncomfortably clear that no such human rights exist and if heaven is to be experienced and eternal life is to be gained, if salvation is to be obtained and forgiveness granted, it will be on the basis of *grace* and not rights! Grace is God giving us what we don't deserve and making it abundantly clear that we don't deserve it!

Kindness is the last of these words that we need to consider. Paul says that the kindness of God is shown toward us in Christ. It was extremely kind of God to even consider sending His Son to our world and even more kind for Him to allow Christ to go through with His task. God was not taken aback by the hostility which Christ met, but fully expected it. It was unbelievably kind of Him to go ahead knowing the end results before He began and to be long-suffering enough to stick with His plan through the sheer agony of the rejection of His Son. He was so kind.

To be treated with mercy and grace, love and kindness, is to be reminded of the beauty of God in sharp contrast to our own ugliness. To be treated this way is to be confronted with the reality of God and man and to take the only position that man can properly take before God. A position of humble gratitude.

What God Did

As a result of God's staggering attitude toward us, according to Paul, He did several things.

First God saved us (v. 8). To be saved means to be liberated or delivered. The New Testament talks about being saved in three tenses. For instance, in

1 Corinthians 1:18 the expression used is, literally, "are being saved." But in Romans 5:9 it is "we shall be saved." However in the verse we are considering, Paul means "you have been saved."

When we put these three together, the result is a full-orbed statement concerning what God has done in the past and has committed Himself to do in the future concerning the deliverance needed by us from sin. We know we will be saved in the future from sin's presence. As far as our past is concerned, we know we have been saved from sin's penalty. And as we grow in our relationship with Him and live in the power of His life we are being saved from sin's power.

Then we note that He quickened us. The phrase used in verse 5, "even when we were dead in sins, hath quickened us together with Christ," means that God made us alive with Christ.

One day while working in my garden, I noticed that someone had left our green watering hose lying in the grass. It looked rather like a 100-foot snake! As I reached down to pick it up it suddenly leaped to life and I leaped to safety! My son had seen me reach for the hose and turned on the water. The hose came alive with water!

Like a hose in the grass, many a person lies spiritually dormant and dead. But the action of God in sending His Spirit into our lives to impart the life of Christ can make a whole life come alive.

Closely related to this is the thought that He raised us (v. 6). When God sends the Spirit of His Son into the life of a forgiven sinner, this not only makes the dead one come alive with Christ, but also raises him to a new position in the heavenlies where *He seated us with Christ* (v. 6). We not only share His life but we share His triumph over the things that formerly triumphed over us, and we share His throne from which He will rule over all.

It doesn't require much spiritual insight to recognize that we are totally incapable of saving ourselves, quickening ourselves, raising ourselves and seating ourselves. But God has done it for those of us who are saved by grace through faith. And for this action in the area of our inadequacy we are eternally and humbly grateful.

What God Designed

Paul wrote "that in the ages to come he might show the exceeding riches of his grace . . . " (v. 7).

God designed that we should be exhibits of His grace for all eternity. If you feel some reaction to the suggestion that God is going to make an exhibition of you, stop reacting because that is exactly what the word "show" means as Paul used it! There is no thought of God embarrassing you for all eternity. Rather you have the privilege of being that which exhibits God's *grace* to all creation.

Some parts of His creation, like the infinite reaches of the galaxies, will be exhibits of His *power*. Others, like the angels, will demonstrate His *holiness*. But only redeemed sinners will be able to show forth His grace. So when a spinning orb wants to understand the grace of God, it will spin in your direction and when you want to see a demonstration of the holiness of God, you'll sit down with a real live angel for a century or two. In eternity all things will have their place showing the many splendored majesty of our

God. But you will be in the *grace* department.

In addition to this, we will be examples of His work-manship. Paul clearly pointed this out in verse 10, "We are his workmanship, created in Christ Jesus unto good works." Francis Foulkes helpfully writes in *The Epistle of Paul to the Ephesians,* "The Greek again gains emphasis by the order of words as it makes the *his* stand first in the sentence."[2] *His* work-manship are we! It is worth noting that the Greek word *poeima* is the root of our word "poem." We are His poem, His creative piece of originality! This, of course, relates to our original creation but also to our re-creation in Christ. We are to be seen as loving evidences of His creative genius, both now and through eternity.

A careful consideration of all these facts will lead us to a humble presenting of ourselves to God in gratitude for His great love and mercy. We will cer-tainly recognize the necessity of a full understanding of these things to deliver us from our lamentable tendency to "boast." But seeing things from God's angle will deliver us from this because we will daily recognize we have an awful lot to be humble about!

Notes

1. William E. Vine, *Expository Dictionary of New Testament Words* (West-wood, NJ: Fleming H. Revell Company, 1940), Vol. 3, p. 60.
2. Francis Foulkes, *The Epistle of Paul to the Ephesians* Tyndale Bible Commentary (London: Tyndale Press; Grand Rapids: Wm. B. Eerdman's Publishing Co., 1963), p. 77.

4

What Do You Say To A Divided World?

Ephesians 2:11-22

One cool, misty day I drove with a group of friends from Tiberias to the top of the Golan Heights. Normally you can see the beautiful Galilean countryside from the heights but that day there was nothing but swirling fog.

We were soon aware of the presence of military forces and burned-out tanks and personnel carriers vividly reminding us of fierce battles fought in the area. We left our vehicle at the forward Israeli positions and walked a few hundred yards through mud and fog till we came to a United Nations encampment. From the top of a small hill we peered eastward through the barbed wire and fortifications to try to see the Syrian positions not far away. But we couldn't see a thing.

I was hit with the irony of the situation. On the Golan Heights is a group of men wearing the blue and white of the United Nations, flying the flag that is recognized around the world and their job is to keep the Israelis and the Syrians apart. Don't miss the irony. United Nations keeping people apart! United but not uniting!

Now I realize that it is as fashionable to be disillusioned with the United Nations as it used to be to scorn the League of Nations between the world wars. But I think it ought to be obvious that there is something wrong when, despite all the expertise and resources of the modern world, all attempts to unite have failed. The best the organizations can do is either give up the unequal struggle as did the league or settle for the role of referee as is the case so often with the U.N.

We have a large share of unresolved international conflicts on the agenda at the moment, such as Ulster and Eire, Zambia and Rhodesia, North and South Korea, Mainland China and Taiwan, just to mention a few. But we should not be blind to the fact that nations have always been at each other's throats and, therefore, if the problem is not new the answers will not be immediate. In fact, the awful truth may be either that there are no answers or there are none to be found in the areas in which society has been looking.

You may be surprised to discover that Paul had something to say on the subject when he wrote to the Ephesians. He used such expressions as enmity, alienated, reconciled, peace and fellow-citizens. He showed clearly that the root of the problem is not primarily nationalistic or even economic but rather moral and spiritual. The answers, therefore, will not be found in the organizations alone.

Jews and Gentiles

One of the traditional divisions in the human race is that which exists between Jew and Gentile. History is replete with appalling evidences of this division and its inhuman outworkings. Of course, it would be foolish to suggest that differences do not exist between Jew and Gentile. But the thing that is so grievous is that the differences have led to division which, in turn, has degenerated into hatred and bloodshed.

Paul clearly spells out the differences. The Jews called themselves the "circumcision" and all those who were not of their number the "uncircumcision." They were perfectly entitled to call themselves by such a title because the special relationship that existed between them and Jehovah was marked by circumcision as God had directed. But there was no real justification for their supercilious use of the term when referring to themselves and their condescending attitude to the "uncircumcision."

In the same way, the Jews had every right to be proud of their special status as members of the "commonwealth of Israel" (v. 12). The word translated "commonwealth" occurs only twice in the New Testament—the other occasion being Paul's statement concerning his Roman citizenship in Acts 22:28. This idea of citizenship in Israel was not so much a political concern. The nations of the world in Paul's time could hardly be expected to get excited about or envious of the state of Israel which had been a shambles for some considerable time.

Paul was thinking more of a spiritual status, as the expression "the covenants of promise" indicates. Actually in the Greek there is a great emphasis in this expression and it should read, "covenants of the promise" relating, of course, to *the* promise made by Jehovah to Abraham and his seed concerning Messiah. But the other people were clearly outside this citizenship and remote from this great promise and the Jews had every intention of keeping it that way. True, they did have means whereby people could become proselytes but the requirements were quite stringent and even if some Gentiles were able to go through the proselytizing process, they were still not made to feel completely at home among the true blue Jews.

Superiority Complex

So the Gentiles were not only outside the special relationship which Jehovah had instituted with Israel but they were made to feel inferior by the Jews who felt extremely superior. As a result, Paul said the Gentiles were "aliens" and "strangers" and "having no hope" and, what is worse, "without God in the world" (v. 12). Estranged from God and made to feel inferior by many a Jew who had become arrogant in his special position, the Gentiles had as little time for the Jews as they had knowledge of God.

The mutual antagonisms existing between Jew and Gentile were understandable but inexcusable. The differences were of God and self-evident, but the divisions were of man and utterly unacceptable.

There is a sense in which the writers of the Declaration of Independence were absolutely right when they said that all men are created equal. Yet it is equally self-evident that major differences exist between man and his fellowman and that some of these differences can be traced directly to God's purposes. This is obviously true in the case of Israel and, to a somewhat lesser extent, in the modern world.

Recently when representatives of 35 countries met in Paris for the Conference on International Economic Cooperation the nations were divided into the North and the South. Those from the North were the industrialized, developed countries and those from the South, the less industrialized and poorer nations. The South wanted a larger slice of the North's pie and the North wanted to keep as much pie as possible.

There was much debate and little agreement on the reasons for the unequal division of pie. But there is no doubt that a major part of the difference is directly attributable to the distribution of natural resources and climatic differences. These differences are related to God's creative choice and divine principle. Nothing that man can do or has done can alter these fundamental differences. But something has to be done about the major divisions that have grown up because of these differences. In the Paris meeting one official told *Time* magazine, "We were within a hair of breakdown. If we had known what a risk we were taking, we might never have started this dialogue."[1] Two weeks later, the same magazine reporting on the meeting of "high officials from the 26-nation Organization of American States" said the "gathering divided bitterly." One observer said, "It's a dialogue of the deaf. No one is listening to the other."[2]

It is apparent to many people that some of the answers to national divisions and personal antagonisms are to be found in the spiritual realm. But to the majority this is not at all clear. Paul's explanation of

God's dealings in the classic Jewish-Gentile confrontation bear careful study and application to the present situation. He told the Ephesians that they had been brought out of their Gentile background and from their Gentile prejudices into a relationship with some of the Jews of Ephesus who had relinquished their untenable attitudes and contemptuous behavior patterns toward the Gentiles. So it can be done! But what does it take?

The Key to Reconciliation

Christ Jesus is the key to the whole remarkable activity of God in reconciliation. It is "in Christ Jesus" (v. 13) that solutions are to be found. To be more explicit, it is "by the blood of Christ" (v. 13) that matters can be resolved.

The prominent place given to the blood of Christ in the bringing together of antagonistic societies shows conclusively that spiritual factors are involved. These spiritual factors include the sinfulness of man and the necessity of forgiveness and cleansing through the only medium available—the blood of Christ. There are those who immediately raise an uproar when spiritual answers are proposed for what they consider to be economic and political problems, and I heartily agree with their reaction. But I also want to do my share of uproar raising against those who fail to see that what they regard as exclusively political and economic problems actually incorporate spiritual aspects.

The Jews had the advantage of divine revelation in greater degree than the Gentiles. Accordingly, when they lived in obedience they prospered greatly. When they accepted divine principle and followed divine direction they were a remarkable people. They could hardly be blamed for their prosperity under such circumstances. The envy and bitterness that their prosperity engendered was sin on the part of the Gentiles as was the greed and the selfishness of the Jews who sought to keep what they had. Sin, which comes as a reaction to differing circumstances, is at the root of our problems today just as it was in days of old. The North is sinning against the South in not sharing and caring enough. The South is sinning against the North in lusting and demanding, hating and maligning.

Jews had sinned, Gentiles had sinned, but both could be forgiven through the blood of Christ. In addition, Christ had come that He "might reconcile both unto God in one body by the cross, having slain the enmity thereby" (v. 16). It is imperative that we do not miss Paul's statement concerning reconciliation to God, because in this passage he shows that reconciliation of man to God and man to man are inextricably bound up in each other. As the enmity which comes from man's sin divides man and God, and enmity between man and man broadens the gulf between them, so the cross of Christ brings everyone before God in humble repentance and confession. Then each turns to the other to repent and confess to each other and seek reconciliation.

Imagine the impact that would have been felt if *Time* had been able to report that the meetings of leaders in Paris concluded with all the politicians humbly confessing the sin of their nations and seeking God's forgiveness. Then, turning to each other, they called their sin sin and began to deal with it as such! Far out? So far out that it will probably never happen. Which is exactly why we will probably not see anything more than fruitless attempts to bridge the gaps that now divide us and may well destroy us.

Old Bones of Contention

"For he is our peace, who hath made both one" (v. 14). In Ephesus He had done it, because both Jew and Gentile had bowed low before the crucified Lord and been united to Him and, in Him, to each other. Of course, the old bones of contention still existed and any realist would recognize that it would only be a matter of time till Jew and Gentile were up to their old hateful ways again.

But the work of Christ goes deeper than that for He also "hath broken down the middle wall of partition . . . even the law of commandments contained in ordinances" (vv. 14,15). In the Temple there was a wall between the Temple court and the court of the Gentiles on which was an inscription which "forbade any foreigner to go in, under pain of death." Perhaps Paul had this in mind when he talked about the partition between the Jew and Gentile. Of course we know that Paul was eventually falsely charged by his own people with taking an Ephesian Gentile, Trophimus, past this sign and into the forbidden court.

The Jews had added many such rules and ordinances to those laid down by God. As a result they had built an imposing structure of regulations that served to increase the gulf between them and the Gentiles. But when Christ came all these things were done away. Those laws that God had ordained till

Christ came were fulfilled in Him. Those laws that men had added were shown to be irrelevant by Him.

In the fulfilling of some of the laws and the exposure of the importance and irrelevance of the others, the bones of contention between Jew and Gentile were taken away and He became their peace. Instead of arguing about rules and regulations and fighting about cultural differences and prejudices, some of the Jews and some of the Gentiles in Ephesus started getting excited about Jesus Christ who had forgiven them all and had shown how the old barriers could be removed. Whenever they got into a fight about culture or tradition thereafter (as they certainly must have done!), it would take only the mention of the name of Christ to bring both sides to a realization of what was really important.

A Brand New Body

If this still sounds ominously impractical and idealistic, remember that the Lord did another magnificent thing when He was able "to make in himself of twain one new man" (v. 15), a slight variation of the phrase "who hath made both one" (v. 14). The impact of these statements is that He made out of two things or peoples one entirely new thing or people. He did not tell both to compromise or even to adjust. His way was not to negotiate at the bargaining table. He called no meeting of Jew and Gentile and gained reluctant concessions from both. Neither did He insist on a reciprocal agreement based on give and take. He simply made something altogether new. He did not Christianize Jews or Judaize Gentiles. He produced no half-breed Ephesian-children-of-Abraham or Abrahamized-children-of-Diana. What horrific monstrosities they would have been, and how similar to many of man's best efforts at reconciliation and negotiation! He made a brand new body called the Body of believers.

It must have been unbelievably hard for traditional Jews to lay their traditions at the foot of the cross and say they were no longer preeminent in their lives. Imagine what must have been involved in an Ephesian laying all the practices of his worship of Diana before the crucified Christ. But Jew and Gentile did such things and found as they did that they had laid aside the things that had divided them and the attitudes that had destroyed all relationship between them. Then they were ready to be made into a new society based on Christ. It was to be composed entirely of forgiven sinners. Its principles were to be the principles of Christ, not the traditions of men. Its dynamic was the grace of God and its end was the glory of God.

Today's societies must not only repent and be reconciled to God and each other but they must also allow Him to take away the "wall of partition." Cultural differences must be examined in the light of the truth of God and evaluated thereby. Instead of being the inviolable principles of societal behavior they must be subordinated to the dictates of Christ. Ideologies must be revamped, political strategies reworked, agreements reexamined and commitments reaffirmed, all before the searching gaze of the risen Lord. Impossible? Not impossible, but highly improbable. Because it would be as hard for the nations of the world to turn from their sin and live unto Christ as it was for the Jew and the Gentile to make the radical commitment in Ephesus. And, as we know that only a minority did it then, we can realistically anticipate little more today.

There Is Something Happening

But there is a work of such radical proportions going on. It is not moving entire nations and revolutionizing whole summit conferences, but God's work is as real in today's world as it was in the needy world of Ephesus. God is building His new society, quietly but relentlessly. This new society of black and white, rich and poor, reprobate and saint, North and South, bond and free, male and female is—you guessed it— the church!

This church has come into being wherever Christ came in the person of His servants and "preached peace." Those who responded to the message of the redeeming, revolutionizing gospel of Christ became "no more strangers and foreigners, but fellow citizens with the saints, and of the household of God" (v. 19).

It's terribly hard for our secularized society to admit it, but there is an alternative society staring them right in the eye. It is challenging their prejudices, calling their bluffs, accepting their challenges and exposing their sins.

The church has her role clearly defined by her Lord. She is to be the "new thing" He has made through His death and resurrection. She is not to be a pale reflection of an anemic Christ or a dull product of outdated dogma. She does not exist to perpetuate tradition and prejudice or to imitate her surrounding society.

She is Christ's new thing! She is one of the greatest arguments for the veracity of her Lord and the viability of His gospel. She can do what nothing else can do and be what no other part of society can possibly be. She, through the work of the Holy Spirit moving in the presentation of the gospel of Christ, is drawing people into a living relationship with God which is recognizable and definable in terms of relationships which transcend every conceivable barrier known to man.

In the church of Christ, there are no such people as "strangers and foreigners," but only "fellow citizens with the saints, and of the household of God" (v. 19). This new community, far from being a holy version of a secular commune or a spiritual adaptation of a psychological therapy group, is based on a much more solid basis and foundation than common needs or shared problems. This community is built "upon the foundation of the apostles and prophets" (v. 20), meaning the revelation of God and His works through the prophetic and apostolic ministries. In sharp and striking contrast to the philosophies and life-styles of the secular world, this new thing of God operates on the timeless revelation of God's truth presented and preserved through the sacred pages of prophetic and apostolic Scripture.

New Society

But in case we think the community is nothing more than a group of dropouts from secular society which peruses ancient writings and follows outdated concepts, Paul adds the momentous truth, "Jesus Christ himself being the chief corner stone" (v. 20).

This is the crux of the new society. The One who redeemed the society and reconciled the redeemed, also resides in the society to be the vital, living force of its existence.

Later in this book we will look further into the wonderful truths that Paul taught concerning the church. Right now we will simply note two stirring statements about the church and try to allow them to sink into our consciousness. The church is "a holy temple in the Lord" and "a habitation of God through the Spirit" (vv. 21,22). Let me remind you that this is no idealistic dream but the hard truth of what God had achieved in Ephesus. Don't forget that He had worked with the raw material of mutually antagonistic Jews and Gentiles. And remember, whatever else you forget, that the presentation of Christ and the building of God's new thing, the church, is what we say to a divided world and what we must demonstrate to a fractured society.

Notes

1. *Time* magazine (June 13, 1977), p. 30.
2. *Time* magazine (June 27, 1977), pp. 7,8.

5

The Inside Story

Ephesians 3:1-13

I sometimes wonder how Paul dictated one of his letters. Did he pace up and down his cell rattling his chains, waving his manacled hands, pouring out sentence after sentence as his amanuensis tried desperately to keep up with him? Or was his dictation slow and deliberate, punctuated by careful reference, deep thought and discussion with whoever was visiting with him at the time? We don't know, but there are certain passages in his epistles which certainly suggest that at times his thoughts sailed into glorious orbit only to touch down after some considerable time.

The early part of Ephesians appears to me to be a case in point as it flows easily and majestically from one eternal concept to another. But after two chapters (as we know them, although they were not dictated with such divisions), the apostle appears to pause briefly. In fact, his sentences become somewhat dis-

61

jointed and his thought less fluid to such an extent that he starts to say something in verse 1 which he promptly forgets and only gets around to in verse 14. "For this cause—" he wrote, and then left the Ephesians (and us) hanging in midair waiting to find out what was on his mind.

But when Paul digressed, he digressed. And as Dr. H.C.G. Moule wrote in his *Ephesian Studies*, "It is a digression quite abnormal on strict rhetorical principles. But it is of a kind which carries with it its own peculiar eloquence and impression." Then he added pointedly, "And where is the parenthesis of St. Paul that does not give the Church some conspicuous treasures of revelation?"[1]

Conspicuous Treasures

So parenthesis and digression notwithstanding, let us examine the conspicuous treasures of the early part of chapter 3! He refers to himself as "the prisoner of Jesus Christ for you Gentiles" (v. 1). In actual fact, he was what E.K. Simpson called a "caged eagle penned within Nero's prison bars."[2] But the fact that he was Nero's prisoner was not important to Paul because he saw himself much more a servant of Christ than a subject of Nero.

Paul's view of himself was such that he was more oriented to his calling than his circumstances, and the people whom he served than the personal consequences of his service. The troubles which led him eventually to Nero's prison bars were closely related to Ephesus because his insistence on opening the doors of God's dealings with man to include Gentiles as well as Jews brought him into increasing conflict with his own people. And when they thought he had taken the Ephesian, Trophimus, into the Temple area where Gentiles were barred, they caused the riot that, one step after another, led Paul to appeal to Caesar and eventually to Rome. So he thought of his imprisonment as the result of serving Jesus Christ in general and the Ephesians in particular. And he was pleased to serve both irrespective of the consequences.

Warming to the theme of his own service, he reminded them that they were fully aware that "the dispensation of the grace of God" (v. 2) had been given to him on behalf of the nations of the world and that he was busy getting on with the fulfillment of this dispensation. You will remember that "dispensation" means a special duty or responsibility. But we need to look closely at his use of the phrase "grace of God."

Paul used the expression sometimes to describe the wonderful attitude of God toward sinners much as John Newton, the slave trader, used it in his well-known hymn, "Amazing Grace." But on other occasions, Paul thought of the grace of God as the daily empowering or enabling that allowed him to serve God out of gratitude for all that He had done. On this occasion, however, it appears that he is thinking of the grace of God as a special act or favor in allowing him to do something for no other reason than God wanted him to do it. Why God wanted Paul to be the apostle to the nations, only God knows. But He is free to choose whom He will and the chosen man will accept the privileges and live with the attendant hardships with an overwhelming sense of being part of the mysterious workings of God.

Why Me?

"Why me?" is the plaintive cry so often uttered by people who do not understand why tragedies and difficulties come their way. "Why me?" ought also to be the continual cry of the converted sinner who knows that God not only saved him by His grace, but gave him a job to do for no other reason than He wants him to do it!

It is fascinating to get Paul's inside story of how God brought him from rabid anti-Christian activities to tireless propagation of the truth as it is in Jesus Christ. But there is another inside story in these verses that is even more fascinating. As we have seen earlier in this book, the term "mystery" was used by Paul differently from our contemporary usage. When Paul talked about the "mystery of Christ" (v. 4) he meant that God had given the inside story on His own mind and purposes. To believe as Paul did that God graciously called him to Himself, then wonderfully chose him to be an apostle and, in addition, showed him things unknown to man but known to God, is to believe that one has a destiny to fulfill and role to play in the affairs of men. This sense of destiny will drive man to unbelievable lengths and enable him to achieve unprecedented things.

History is full of the stories of men and women who have come on the human stage at a certain time in the economy of God to achieve things for God and man that must be achieved. Hudson Taylor, regarded by some of his missionary colleagues as a nobody, showed that in God's plans for China he was somebody.

Apparently unperturbed by the way his colleagues

were decidedly underwhelmed by him, Taylor went ahead and did things his critics did not achieve, and accomplished things that no other man had been able to accomplish. The motivation for this service was a tremendous sense of calling and destiny. If he had needed the help and encouragement and continual plaudits of man in order to function, he would never have got started. But he was able to work with great efficiency because he had discovered something of his place in God's mind and will for the Chinese. It would seem to me to be self-evident that a greater sense of what God is doing and where we personally fit into His doing of it would be of immeasurable value to the contemporary church.

Mystery of Christ

But I have digressed as did our great apostle! To return to the expression "the mystery of Christ," we need to remember that it refers to the revelation of God's purposes for mankind in the person and work of Jesus Christ. Paul said that he had already introduced these truths "in few words" (v. 3) presumably referring to the early parts of the Epistle.

But Paul adds further information at this point which is important to our understanding of the plan of God for the Ephesians. This revelation, revealed as it was through the "holy apostles and prophets by the Spirit" (v. 5), had not been available in such detail to former generations but was now clearly shown. The mystery was, in short, that God had chosen to make Gentiles "fellow heirs, and of the same body, and partakers of his promise in Christ" (v. 6).

In a sense there was nothing new about this revelation because, while it was true that God had specially chosen the children of Israel to be His people, He had made it perfectly clear that in Abraham all the nations of the earth would be blessed. God had never shared the limited view of His purposes that His children held. But at the same time, the nations of the world had been strangers and aliens to the intimate revelation of what God had for them until Christ came and "preached peace" to them that were "afar off, and to them that were nigh" (2:17).

God's plan is to gather to Himself, in Christ, people from every conceivable area of this world, every people, every culture, every age and make them one. All barriers are to go, all divisions to be resolved, gulfs bridged, wars resolved. The incompatible are to be made compatible; the irreconcilable reconciled. Proud separatist Jews will open hearts and minds to Gentile dogs; hostile, hateful Gentiles will embrace despised Jews; and Christ will be the Prince of peace, the One who alone can bring man together.

Keep It in the Future

Many people believe this and are perfectly happy about it. But they believe that it will all take place at some great and glorious future date and, therefore, they should not allow such truths to interfere with their life-styles before the great day. So they feel quite comfortable being prejudiced, separatist saints. They see no inconsistency in being part of the Body of Christ that embraces all manner of people, yet, at the same time, refusing to have any kind of fellowship with other parts of the Body.

Another deeply perturbing fact of contemporary

church life is that, in so many gatherings of God's people, there appears to be little interest in making sure that people of every nation are alerted to the international and interracial nature of the plan of God for His church. Through the years there has been traditionally a missionary concern in some areas of the church but it was usually confined to a small minority. Financial support for the propagation of the mystery of God is usually rated behind numerous other concerns and priorities. Many churches exhibit little concern that they have produced few people in their congregations who have gone to the far corners of the world to share the mystery of Christ.

The problem is not confined to the churches of the Western world. In many countries where there has been a church for more than 100 years, through the effective ministries of missionaries, it is sad to observe the apparent lack of concern on the part of the church people for those who do not know Christ. I was told of evangelical believers in South America who had no interest in reaching the primitive Indians in the jungles of their own countries. If the Indians were to be reached, the American missionaries could do it. The missionaries told me, personally, that many of the believers in the churches doubted if the primitive Indians have souls! Few believers I have met would go so far or stoop so low, but many show no greater understanding of God's purposes for the world and exhibit no more interest in being part of the practical outworking of such a plan.

Minister of the Mystery

Perhaps part of the problem is that we lack the

attitude of the apostle Paul which is clearly demonstrated by the things he told the Ephesians about
himself and his ministry. He said that he had been
made a "minister" of this mystery (v. 7). The word
he used is really "servant," a revealing word.

The Lord Jesus clearly stated in word and demonstrated in action that He had come to serve, not to be
served. This is, of course, a most unusual attitude
because, as we well know, most people naturally enjoy being in on the getting rather than the giving end
of a transaction and most of us are more interested
in having our needs met than our ministries fulfilled.

There is, in our contemporary society, a great emphasis on rights. This may well be perfectly right but
when rights are stressed at the expense of respon-
sibilities, society becomes warped in outlook and in-
effective in action. This has happened in the church
to such an extent that many who profess to be disciples of Christ show little understanding or interest in
adopting the "mind of Christ." Instead of being committed to serve, they are devoted to being served. The
obvious result is that less and less is being achieved
by fewer and fewer people as more and more demands are made upon the overburdened by the uninvolved.

Perhaps we can paraphrase Churchill's words,
"Never in the history of the Christian church have so
many expected so much of so few." And, "Never in
the history of Christian ministry have so few done so
little to reach so many." We desperately need to see
that a fundamental part of Christian experience is
directly related to the servant attitude demonstrated
by our Lord and perpetuated by His apostle.

How to Be Humble

Not only did Paul have the servant attitude but he also had a great sense of humility about his total position and standing before God. The translators had a little problem with the word Paul used to describe himself because it was so unusual. They settled for "less than the least" (v. 8). Paul chose not to use "little" *(mikros)* or "less" *(elatton)* or even "least" *(elachistos)*. He went all the way and called himself *elachistoteros* which the Nestle Marshall R.S.V. translates as "leaster" and adds the footnote, "This is quite literal!—the apostle coins a word."[3] Now that's what I call humility!

Humility has to be learned by most people and the lesson can be painful. Recently, I was talking to a young man who is, by far, the best racquetball player in his club. He is so good that he doesn't beat his opponents, he annihilates them. One day the national champion came to the club and to the delight of many he proceeded to dish out a thorough beating to the local champion. A very humbling situation!

Anyone who is really aware of what God is doing, and how He proposes to do it through human beings, cannot fail to be humbled. When we poke around in the local clubs of our little concepts we can produce a lot of adulation that will promote a deal of pride. But when we stand alongside what He has for us we have little problems deciding with Paul that the words "little," "less," and "least" won't do. We need "leaster" to describe how we feel about our mission.

Three Immense Things

Paul recognized that he was required to preach

what he called the "unsearchable riches of Christ" (v. 8) and "to make all men see what is the fellowship [better "dispensation"] of the mystery" (v. 9). Then he went further and added that the end of this activity was that the church should demonstrate to the "principalities and powers in heavenly places . . . the manifold wisdom of God" (v. 10).

There are three immense things that obviously weighed heavily on the mind of the apostle. First, the immense scope of the message that God has for the world in Christ. Paul calls it "unsearchable" *(anexichiaston)*, a word which Foulkes says means literally "cannot be traced out by human footprints."[4] The same word is used by Paul in Romans 11:33, "How unsearchable are his judgments, and his ways past finding out!" So when a man knows that he is commissioned to learn of God things that can never be adequately grasped by man, and then to seek to make them graspable, he gets very humble quickly.

Then there is the immensity of the task of making "all men see" (v. 9). In Paul's day there was, of course, nothing like the population that we have today; but neither was there a church anything like as large as today. But Paul's era and ours have one thing in common in this respect. We are both faced with an overwhelming task. And while there are many causes for thanksgiving for work well done and major victories won, there is no cause for triumphalism when we consider how many of the "all men" have not the remotest idea of the mystery of Christ.

Heavenly TV
Then there is the strange and wonderful thought

that Paul expressed when he said that the church would be an expression of the "manifold wisdom" of God to a watching heavenly host (v. 10). The church has a far bigger viewing audience than anybody realizes. I have often noticed the transformation that comes over young athletes when they see a television cameraman standing on the sidelines. They play just that little bit harder. But they exert even more effort if they ever get the chance to play in a game being televised nationwide.

Imagine, therefore, the concern in Paul's heart when he tells the people of Ephesus that they are not on local TV or national TV or even international TV by satellite, but on heavenly TV being watched closely by the heavenly forces.

If this seems a little ridiculous let me remind you that God has a great desire to be known by all His creation. All parts of His creation are limited in their capacity to understand certain aspects of the divine Being. Obviously humans are limited in their grasp of heavenly realms but that is no problem to heavenly beings. But heavenly beings have no concept of the hatreds and bitterness of mankind, the feuds and the wars. They don't know what it is to be forgiven and reconciled so they have little concept of God as a gracious forgiver and reconciler. But God wants them to see Him in these capacities. Otherwise their knowledge of Him will be seriously deficient. Hence, the necessity for the church to appear as a living illustration of the remarkable working of God in this respect.

"The manifold wisdom of God" is to be seen at work in the church that God has created. The word translated "manifold" *(polupoikilos)* was used by the translators of the *Septuagint* to describe Joseph's famous coat of many colors. And ancient Greek writers like Homer used it to describe the beauty and variety to be found in flowers. Peter also used a related word to describe "the manifold grace of God" (1 Pet. 4:10) when he was explaining the different ways God equips people to do His work.

So in the church it is the expression of the many and varied ways that God reaches and touches people that is of such interest to the heavenly viewers. The multitude of reconciliations He effects, the varied ways He does it, the different people He touches, the different fellowships He establishes, the various ministries He blesses all show the manifold wisdom and grace of God.

To be confronted with such immense concepts of Christian service as these can be totally destructive to the would-be servant unless he is also alert to the resources for service made available to him through the same Lord who initiated the whole scenario. Paul was deeply aware of this and spoke of "boldness and access ... by faith" (v. 12) into all that God had shown Him. This came from a great conviction that He had received the "gift of the grace of God ... by the effectual working of his power" (v. 7). Later in the Epistle he returns to these themes and we shall look into them at that point. Suffice it to say at this juncture that he knew he could be humble and bold at the same time because he was totally dependent on the One who had called him and shown him the inside story. But he knew that this One was far more committed to the plan being worked out than he was and, therefore, could be trusted to equip and empower those who would humbly serve Him.

To the extent that we have been given a glimpse of the inside story of both God's universal plan and the specific way in which individuals are to be involved in bringing it to pass, we have been enriched and are accordingly more responsible. So all that remains to be said is that as we grasp the inside story, in general, let's find out our part in the implementation of it and then get out there on the big cold outside and let more people into the good news of what God is doing.

Notes

1. H.C.G. Moule, *Ephesian Studies* (London: Hodder and Stoughton, 1900), p. 109.
2. E.K. Simpson and Frederick F. Bruce, *Commentary on the Epistles to the Ephesians and Colossians* (Grand Rapids: Wm. B. Eerdmans Publishing Co., 1957), p. 70.
3. Neštle Marshall R.S.V., *International Greek English New Testament* (London: Samuel Bagster and Sons Ltd., 1968), p. 764.
4. Francis Foulkes, *The Epistle of Paul to the Ephesians* Tyndale Bible Commentary (London: Tyndale Press; Grand Rapids: Wm. B. Eerdman's Publishing Co., 1963), p. 96.

6

When Is A Cell A Prayer Cell?

*Ephesians 3:14-21*_____

Some people go to prison as rank amateurs and come out skilled professionals. Others use the time more profitably. John Bunyan, imprisoned over a period of 12 years in the seventeenth century, wrote his masterpiece, *The Pilgrim's Progress*, during the long cold days of his incarceration. More recently Ferdinand Marcos, imprisoned in his native Philippines, studied law with such success that he chose to defend himself against the charge of murder and was acquitted. Subsequently he became president.

Paul used his time wisely too. We know of his prison epistles, including the letter to the Ephesians, and we have information concerning his evangelistic activities with such notables as Agrippa and Felix. There are accounts of him receiving people for various ministries and, of course, his vocal efforts at Philippi are well known. But we should not overlook his prayer life in the cell.

Given as Paul was to a life-style of great activity

and fervor it is fascinating to notice his great emphasis on prayer. It may have been that he didn't get around to praying as much when he was outside as when he was behind bars, but there is no question about the place that prayer played in his prison cell.

We have already spent time looking into the first prayer which he incorporated into his Epistle and now we find that his mind returns once again to this noble and necessary spiritual exercise. At the beginning of the chapter he started to tell the Ephesians that his great grasp of God's wonderful plan and activity led him to pray for them but then he was diverted to other things by the fullness of his fertile mind. Eventually, however, he repeated the phrase, "for this cause" (v. 14), but this time he managed to keep going without being interrupted by his own thoughts.

A Matter of Posture

"I bow my knees unto the Father" may appear to be a singularly unimportant expression to us, particularly if we habitually kneel to pray by our beds or in specially padded pews in church. But Jewish men usually didn't kneel to pray. They stood up! Anyone who has been to Jerusalem will have been strangely moved by the crowds of men standing at the Wall swaying and rocking on the balls of their feet, all the time reading their prayers. That was how Paul would traditionally pray, but for some reason he had changed his posture.

On the relatively few occasions that Scripture records people kneeling to pray, it is noticeable that deep emotion of an extraordinary nature was related to the incident. For instance, when Solomon's Temple was dedicated the king knelt (see 2 Chron. 6:13); when the Lord was in the Garden of Gethsemane he "kneeled down, and prayed" (Luke 22:41); and when Paul said his farewells to the Ephesian elders on the seashore he "kneeled down, and prayed with them all" (Acts 20:36). So we are probably right in assuming that Paul was deeply moved at this point of his dictation and slipped to his knees to respond to the things he had been sharing.

This I find to be very challenging. How rare it is for people to be driven to their knees by nothing other than a consideration of what God has said! In many instances it is impossible to get people to be alert to what God is saying even when they take the trouble to come out to a church service. They give the impression that the whole thing is something of a bore and their ill-disguised yawns and barely-concealed glances at their watches after the first 20 minutes of the sermon show that whatever else happens they will not be sinking to their knees when the exposition is complete! As a preacher of the Word, I also search my own heart concerning my attitude to the things that God has shown me and wonder so often how I can be so little moved by the immensity of His grace and the majesty of His cosmic plan.

Father of All Fathers

Part of the reason for our relative (or absolute) prayerlessness is that we have no real understanding of the mechanics and dynamics of prayer. Some people feel rather stupid talking either to the ceiling or repeating muffled phrases into their bed covers. Paul however had no such problem. He knew he was praying to "the Father, from whom every family in heaven and on earth is named" (vv. 14,15, *RSV*).

New Testament manuscripts vary somewhat at this point and commentators are not agreed on the exact meaning of Paul's words. His expression *pasa patria* is obviously related to the word *pater* which even if we know little Greek will be recognizable as the word for father. So in effect, he is talking about the Father of all "father related" societies. Moule suggests "father's family or father's house." Foulkes uses such words as "lineage, pedigree, tribe or nation."[2] While Simpson expresses his thought with the phrase "Father of all fatherhoods."[3]

From this brief review two things become apparent. First, there is some degree of uncertainty and, second, there is no doubt that Paul believed that in every area where fatherhood is experienced, however inadequately, there is some demonstration of the attitude of God to His people.

I am the father of three teenagers. They bring all manner of joys and stresses to bear in my family. But I have discovered that whatever the situation may be, as a father, I have a deep concern for the well-being of my children and a deep desire to assist them in the often traumatic business of growing up. I am conscious of many paternal limitations (partly due to the helpful exposure of my wife and children!). But despite the limitations, there are at least some indications of what fatherhood is all about.

The Father in heaven is the ultimate in fatherhood and is at very least concerned about the well-being of His children and committed to the growth of their experience. As such He is eminently approachable.

And in the understanding of this lies one of the great lessons of prayer. Far from being dwarfed by the divine transcendence, Paul was drawn by the divine fatherhood. He loved to talk to the Father because he knew He was concerned and available.

A Matter of Style

Another great aspect of prayer that is so often overlooked is the resources from which God can and does answer prayer. To come before an impoverished, disinterested being with requests however moving and valid is only to invite disappointment and futility. But to come to One who gives "according to" (not "out of") "the riches of his glory" (v. 16), is to anticipate great things.

I point out the difference between "according to" and "out of" because it is important. A multimillionaire who gives a dime is giving "out of his riches," but hardly "according to" his riches. Moule delightfully paraphrases "according to . . . , on the scale and in the style of."[4] God, you will be thrilled to know, does the latter!

We have seen something of the attitude of the apostle as he kneels in his cell. We know he has a great sense of freedom in prayer because he recognizes God as his Father, and a tremendous sense of anticipation because he recognizes that God gives in a way that is consistent with His eternal resources. Now it is time to look at the specific requests that he made.

There is a different emphasis in this prayer from the prayer of the first chapter. Sidlow Baxter, in *Explore the Book*, wrote, "The prayer in chapter 1 was that we might KNOW. This prayer in chapter 3 is that we might HAVE."[5]

The first request is for strength. There is no surprise in this, for I am sure all of us who have followed Paul this far in his exposition of what God is doing will be feeling decidedly weak-kneed about the part that we are to play. There is, in my experience, nothing more designed to show me my weakness than a clear presentation of the divine expectation!

The more I see the possibilities from God's perspective the more I recognize the necessities of God's dynamic enabling. Not only possibility but there is also the opportunity, and privilege, and responsibility! What an opportunity is mine! Whenever I think of this I am reminded of the boy who, having fallen into a barrel of molasses, was heard to pray, "Lord, make my capacity equal to this opportunity!" So whichever way we look at the truth revealed so far there will be a great desire for strength in all those who seek to enter more fully into all that God is doing.

The details of this strengthening are quite straightforward. It will be superlative because we are to be "strengthened with might," it will be supernatural because it is related to activity of the Holy Spirit, and it will take place in the innermost recesses of the "inner man" (v. 16). Paul's delight in multiplying phrases to try to express the majestic scope of God's activity is once again in evidence as he talks about "strengthened with might." The words used in the Greek speak of different kinds of power and enabling and when added together give a great sense of something quite extraordinary.

The Holy Spirit is well known as the means of making power available to redeemed people. It is He who takes us from the area of intellectual appreciation of the power available to Christians, as illustrated in the prayer of chapter 1, into the experimental knowledge of power actually and really at work in our lives. So often I hear Christians respond to messages from the Word of God with the words, "That's all very well, but—" They then begin a recital of reasons why the principles outlined and the admonitions given, which they wholeheartedly accept, cannot be expected to work in their lives. This indicates a lack of basic comprehension of the fact that the Holy Spirit is a Person whose power is to be reckoned with. He, having worked in the believer's life in bringing clarification and conviction and regeneration, is as mighty on the believer's behalf in bringing spiritual strength into the "inner man."

To talk in this way is to deal to a certain extent with apparently abstract concepts. Yet there is ample concrete evidence of the Holy Spirit's power in the "inner man" as Paul's personal testimony showed. He said that while the "outer," by which he meant his physical body, was being destroyed, the "inner" was daily renewed (see 2 Cor. 4:16). He explained this so that the Corinthians would know how he could be so resilient and persistent in the midst of unbelievably difficult and often dangerous circumstances. How was he able to sing in prison with a bleeding back? Because while the "outer" was taking a beating the "inner" was getting a refreshing! How could he return to a city from which he had just been dragged after a stoning? Because while the stones were bashing the life from the "outer" the Spirit was pouring His life in the "inner." This is the kind of strength the Holy Spirit gives and this was what he longed for in the Ephesian church and if he were around today, I am sure he would pray it for us, too.

The second request is for love. Remember that Paul had heard of their faith and love to all the saints and in fact had given thanks for this in the early part of the first prayer (1:15). But he knew that no saint has ever exhausted the possibilities of love and that there is a long way for even the most loving believer to go in the experience of loving relationships.

We have seen how Paul in his enthusiasm sometimes forgot to finish what he had started to say and how on other occasions he was perfectly happy making up words if he felt that an adequate term was not available. He had another encouraging and charming characteristic. He was not averse to an occasional mixed metaphor!

My old English teacher's stock illustration of mixed metaphors was the story of the British parliamentarian who reputedly said one day, "Mr. Speaker, I smell a rat; I see him forming in the air and darkening the sky; but I'll nip him in the bud." Paul wasn't quite that bad (or good), but he did talk about people growing like trees and being built like buildings in the same breath when he said that he wanted them to be "rooted and grounded in love" (v. 17). We must not let his literary peculiarities detract from his inspired theological revelation. But it is encouraging to see that the Holy Spirit works in people as they are and His work is not at all diluted by their shortcomings.

To be thoroughly grounded and based on love was another consequence of being empowered by the Spirit. But, as we have already seen, the work of the Spirit is essentially practical. So the idea of being a person whose life-style and substance are based and rooted in love is to be taken seriously. We are to look seriously at our lives to see to what extent the fruits on the branches show the soil wherein the roots lie. We are to examine the highest point of the life we are erecting to see in what way it demonstrates the foundation upon which the structure stands. The little things and the big things, whether the smallest fruit on a twig or the roof on a building, indicate the fundamental root and foundation of the whole. If love is to be shown in the big and the small the choice of the believer is to live in the power of the Spirit with love as the basic ingredient.

The extent of this love is seen in Paul's dramatic use of the dimensions of "breadth, and length, and depth, and height" (v. 18) which he prays the Ephesians might comprehend.

W.E. Vine explains the word Paul used as follows: "*Katalambano* properly signifies to lay hold of; then, to lay hold of so as to possess as one's own, to appropriate."[6] There is a tendency for all of us to approach biblical truth like kids watching the Fourth of July fireworks. Lots of ohs and ahs in response to a myriad, blinding, glorious heavenly flashes. But Paul will have none of this. He wants this love in all its dimensions to be apprehended, not just appreciated.

Ever the practical man Paul gives two beautiful insights into the way it will work. It will come in the degree in which "Christ may dwell in your hearts by faith" (v. 17), and as it is experienced "with all saints" (v. 18). On the one hand he stresses once again the absolute necessity of the indwelling enabling of God, although this time, instead of talking of the strength of the Holy Spirit, he points to the indwelling presence of the living Christ. This is a different angle on the same truth.

We should not try to differentiate between the indwelling presence of Christ by His Spirit and the indwelling Spirit of Christ. There is, however, one obvious advantage in thinking of the indwelling One as being the living Lord Jesus. Whenever we feel that the concept of "spirit" is too vague and ethereal we can think of the same Lord who walked the Middle East living again in me in the Midwest (or wherever!). There is nothing vague about that. He really lives in the power of His resurrection in the humblest saints in response to their faith.

Paul uses a word that speaks quite forcibly of the permanent nature of this indwelling. He sees Christ living in their lives on a permanent basis through faith. And from His flowing life Paul recognizes the possibilities of really laying hold of love as the basis of life.

Then he mentioned something else that can be easily overlooked. This "love" experience is not for those who live in splendid isolation. Those who withdraw either into monastic seculsion or separatistic individualism may have love as a concept but they cannot have it as a reality, for the simple reason that you can't love in the abstract or in isolation. It takes community both to learn and to express love. Hence the absolute necessity for believers to be operating in the context of a fellowship where love is both poured out and drunk in.

Without the varied relationships of a larger community, love becomes selfish and selfish love is a contradiction in terms. Life without relationships becomes limited. And that is the opposite of apprehending the love of Christ in all the dimensions Paul listed. So as we live, trusting the One who permanently lives within and practically giving and taking love in the community of saints, things will happen that will be beyond our capacity to explain. Even Paul came to the limits at this point and wrote the marvelously paradoxical phrase, "to know the love of Christ, which passeth knowledge" (v. 19). This is a great word for all those who, for various mistaken reasons, think they have arrived.

Always remember that when you get into the experience of knowing the love of Christ, however far you get, you have only begun. It's rather like taking a swim in the ocean. You can thrill to the power of it, relax in the warmth of it, float in the buoyancy of it and taste the salt of it, but you will never measure the extent of it. So go ahead and swim and experience all you can, but please don't give anyone the impression that you have really got the ocean in a bottle!

The third request is for fullness. Paul asks the Father that the Ephesians might be "filled with all the fulness of God" (v. 19). At first sight this request might appear to border on the ridiculous. "How," we might well ask ourselves, "can Paul expect anybody to be filled with all that God is? If that happened it would be like putting a Boeing 747 engine in a Volkswagen. God would just blow the person apart."

Since many people have arrived at this conclusion almost immediately after they have read the words, there has been a sad tendency to relegate this request to the pending file labeled, *PAUL, requests of: unrealistic!*

But wait a minute! What was Paul really saying? "The fulness of God" means all the attributes of God. So far he has talked about knowledge and strength and love, all of which are divine attributes, but at this point he throws everything into one great phrase and asks that they might be filled with all the divine attributes.

So that we might not leave this request out in the mists of never, never land, let us remember that Christ was described by Paul as being the One in whom "all fulness dwells" (Col. 1:19) and he added, "In him dwelleth all the fulness of the Godhead bodily" (Col. 2:9). Put together, these verses tell us that the full attributes of God were shown in bodily form in Christ; therefore the fullness of God is readily recognizable as the character and attitude and disposition of Christ. It is with this quality of life and experience that he wants us to be filled.

But what does he mean by the word filled? Moule quotes the *Cambridge Bible* at this point as follows: "No fanatical rhetoric is here, nor the least dream of a mingling and confusion of the finite and the Infinite . . . the idea is of a vessel connected with an abundant source external to itself, and which will be filled up to its capacity, if the connection is complete."[7] This is helpful for it shows that Paul is praying that people may experience more of the attributes of God (as made clear in Christ) in terms of their own personality and within the confines of their own capacity. Now we all know something of the limitation and confines of our own personality, but the prayer is that within those limits the living God might show His love and power and wisdom and grace.

This does not mean that I will cease to be me. It does not suggest that you will have to be like me. But it does mean that both of us will still be recognizable as ourselves, yet, at the same time, will demonstrate similar characteristics, the characteristics of Christ Himself. For example take a man and wife. Probably she will demonstrate feminine characteristics and he masculine. Does the fullness of God make both of them so divine that they become human neuters? Of course not, it means that godliness and manliness will be demonstrated by the one and godliness and womanliness in the other. Will old people and young people become nondescript middleaged divine machines? Not at all. Both will show the nature of Christ, the one in terms of elderly serenity, the other in terms of youthful vigor.

To make absolutely certain that there should be no lingering doubts about the realism of this prayer, Paul concludes with a great doxology to the One of whom he is making the requests. This wonderful Lord is described as Him who "is able to do exceeding abundantly above all that we ask or think" (v. 20), so there shouldn't be any problem in the possibilities of getting answers. Even if we think Paul was aiming a little too high, remember that the Lord can do "exceeding abundantly above" anything even Paul could think. So the possibilities are there and it is for His glory that the requests are made.

I don't know how you feel after working through a prayer like this one, but personally I feel like a small boy standing on the edge of the ocean, looking into the sunset and saying, "Lord, you made both ocean and sunset and they are beautiful and vast. You also made me and I'm neither. But I'm part of what you're doing, so take me and bathe me with the sunset tones of your grace and plunge me into the ocean depths of your Being, so that in terms of my frail inadequacy, you will be shown in your fullness."

Maybe you feel the same. I hope so!

Notes

1. H.C.G. Moule, *Ephesian Studies* (London: Hodder and Stoughton, 1900). p. 128.
2. Francis Foulkes, *The Epistle of Paul to the Ephesians* Tyndale Bible Commentary (London: Tyndale Press; Grand Rapids: Wm. B. Eerdman's Publishing Co., 1963), p. 101.
3. E.K. Simpson and Frederick F. Bruce, *Commentary on the Epistles to the Ephesians and Colossians* (Grand Rapids: Wm. B. Eerdmans Publishing Co., 1957), p. 79.
4. Moule, *Ephesian Studies*, p. 129.
5. J. Sidlow Baxter, *Explore the Book* (London: Marshall, Morgan and Scott, 1951), Vol. 6, p. 176.
6. William E. Vine, *Expository Dictionary of New Testament Words* (London: Lowe and Brydone Limited, 1940), Vol. 1, p. 70.
7. Moule, *Ephesian Studies*, p. 141.

7

Now
For
Something
Totally
Different

*Ephesians 4:1-13*_____

Having arrived at the beginning of the fourth chapter, we have come to the turning point of the Epistle. So far we have been led to the source of all spiritual life. Paul has turned our eyes on the God of the ages, His eternal Son and blessed Holy Spirit. We have seen His plan, heard His call, sensed His power and felt His love. To what end? To the end that we might draw from these resources and live worthily.

This life, which Paul describes as a "walk," surely reminds us that spiritual experience is not the isolated hour on the Lord's day or the mammoth step in occasional mountaintop experiences, but rather the ongoing progression of life in Christ, one simple, practical step after another. To be sure, as in ordinary walks, some steps will be greater than others and a few will be harder than others and some will lead to higher ground than others.

But the spiritual life is a walk and there is a moral responsibility about this walk that is directly related to the source of our life. This we see from Paul's use of the word "therefore" (4:1). Because of the source and the resources, the call and the plan through which we are identified with Christ, there must now be a willingness to progress daily in a way that is compatible with the call and the profession. Note that the remainder of the Epistle is not dry ethical teaching related to ponderous theology. It is an impassioned plea for behavior rightly related to the experience of Christ dwelling in the heart and the God who can do "exceeding abundantly above all that we ask or think."

Community of Saints

We have seen the tremendous emphasis that Paul placed on the community of believers. He firmly believed that one of the great works of God is to bring the incompatible together and enable them to live harmoniously and lovingly. He talked about the Lord Jesus who not only brings those who are at enmity with God into peaceful relationship with Him, but also "preached peace" (2:17) to those who were far from each other and brought them together. It is a sad testimonial to our evangelical myopia that all too often we put such stress on a personal relationship with God through Christ that we almost totally neglect the relationship that must exist between those who are God's children because of Christ.

The necessity for this community of saints in a local geographical location is possibly greater at this time in human history than any other. So many factors are at large in our contemporary world that are having a fragmenting effect on society that many people feel there is a real danger of total societal disintegration. Among other things our society needs a model of functioning society. God calls this society the church and He is committed to its operation because it is as much a part of His plan for mankind as are individual relationships with Him. Our world may have no idea of where to look for a society that builds bridges instead of barriers and operates on the basis of service rather than selfishness, but those who know Christ know.

So it comes as no surprise that Paul starts off his practical application of spiritual truth by showing that believers must live richly in their Christian community. This, he points out, will require such unusual, unnatural qualities as "lowliness and meekness, with long-suffering, forbearing one another in love" (v. 2).

Perhaps you may be tempted at this point to say, "I thought we were getting to the practical part of the Epistle. But here we go talking about all the things I don't have!"

The answer to that must be, "If you don't have them, then it is your responsibility to get them and the Lord Jesus is your indwelling resource to make sure that you do!" This of course does not mean that you just open some internal spiritual valve and all the lowliness and meekness and forbearing of Christ will come gushing into you. It is certainly necessary for you to live in touch with His resources, but it is also vital that you engage in activities that will demand your full cooperation with Him. Paul expresses it by using the word *spoudazontes*, which the *Theological Dictionary of the New Testament* defines as "to push on with something quickly, assiduously, zealously" and "to get seriously involved."[1]

Unity in Community

This earnest effort which draws constantly on the indwelling Christ is designed to "keep the unity of the Spirit in the bond of peace" (v. 3). Every effort must be made earnestly and enthusiastically to maintain the unity that already exists among believers because of the work of God in Christ. This is the strength of the word "keep." We are not asked to manufacture nonexistent unity for that would be an exercise in futility. But we are exhorted to protect and zealously develop the unity existing because of our common experience of Christ.

Warming to his theme the apostle then gives a list of seven aspects of this divinely created unity which already exists among believers. "There is one body, and one Spirit, even as ye are called in one hope of your calling; one Lord, one faith, one baptism, one God and Father of all, who is above all, and through all, and in you all" (vv. 4-6).

There is "one body." God has worked in individual lives and brought them into a relationship with each other of which they may not be aware. This relationship is described by Paul as being similar to that which exists between members of the same body. There is an absolute interdependence and complete unity of being. The body of believers in any one place is an organism which exists, as physical bodies exist, to function as a spiritual being in a physical environment. In the same way that my spiritual existence can be real in the U.S.A. or the Far East through *my body*, so the existence of the ascended Lord is made real in the U.S.A. or the Far East through the being of *the body*. This high concept of Christian experi-

91

ence should be enough to make believers abhor anything that would either hinder the body's function or encourage its malfunction.

There is "one spirit." As we have already seen, every believer has an experience of the Holy Spirit which includes His indwelling. The Holy Spirit is truly resident in every redeemed sinner. This fact, easy to accept academically but desperately difficult to acknowledge practically, is nevertheless part of that which God has already accomplished.

We are well aware that the Holy Spirit among other things works in the life of the believer to stimulate us to a life of obedience and to be the very dynamic of that obedient life-style. It is hard to believe that He will stimulate people to harshness and encourage them in division. So whenever these things emerge in Christian relationships it ought to be evident that the Holy Spirit has been left out of it and He must be called in immediately, for He is the common denominator of all valid Christian motivation.

"You are called in one hope of your calling." One aspect of Christian truth that has been available to the world for centuries is suddenly coming to the attention of the secular world. Since Freud, society has been convinced that the reasons for man's behavior, and therefore the causes of his problems, lie in the past. So we spend countless hours and dollars in analysis.

In more recent times emphasis has been placed on existential ideas which insist that reality is found in any particular action at any given moment, and that the origins of that action in the past and the consequences of the action in future are not important. All that is important is what is happening right now.

The obvious deficiencies of these approaches have become increasingly apparent. So more and more people are looking away from their Freudian past and their existential present to the unknown future. They are going so far as to say that if man has no hope he will not function.

This is where Christians continue to say what they have been saying all along. Those who are called of God to be His children and His servants are confident that He will perfect what He started and complete what He planned. Therefore they are future-oriented people who share the great and glorious hope that Christ will return and bring to consummation all the purposes of God, and they will be part of them. Believers who really believe this tend to concentrate more on their ultimate hope than the differences of their traditional past or the variations of their existential present. Thus they avoid many potentially divisive situations. To put it bluntly, they know they'll be together for all eternity so they have started practicing!

There is "one Lord" (v 5). There is a beautiful story in the Old Testament about David. When he was on the run from Saul, he took refuge in the Cave of Adullam. He was not there very long before people began to arrive to join him. We are not told what their motivation was but we do know that they were not the most impressive group of men. They are described as those who were "in distress, in debt and discontented" (1 Sam. 22:1,2). However, they became a force to be reckoned with and later some of them were known as David's mighty men.

93

We might well ask what it was that could change this unlikely bunch of social outcasts and misfits into a fine force of motivated men. The answer is simple— David "became a captain over them" (1 Sam. 22:2). Their differences and inadequacies became secondary to the strength of his character and the importance of his mission. He was able to win them to himself so thoroughly that their eyes were on him and then on each other. They saw each other not so much as potential threats, competitors or enemies, but as comrades in arms united by their one Lord. So it is with Christ and His people.

There is "one faith." The New Testament talks about faith in two different ways. Sometimes it shows faith to be the attitude of trust and dependence by which people are saved and go on to live the life of the saved. But on other occasions "the faith" appears to be what Foulkes calls, "the same vital truths concerning Him and His work and purpose."[2] In other words there are certain things about the Lord Jesus and His work on which all believers agree, while there are many things on which they differ widely and sometimes wildly. Paul's point is that there are some things on which we build our life of faith in Christ and these things are great and glorious. So while we do not close our eyes to differences or our minds to developments, neither do we close our hearts to those who trust Christ as we do.

There is "one baptism." Of all the things Paul says unite believers, the one most likely to raise eyebrows (and hackles) is "one baptism." The ingenuity of man's interpretation of the Bible's teaching on baptism can be seen in the wide variety of doctrines and modes, denominations and squabbles that have developed over the years. However, through all the confusion I think it would be true to say that all believers see baptism in one way or another as a rite of identification with the Lord Jesus. We recognize it to be something that He expects of His church and that His disciples should identify with Him in this way. So a unifying factor here, even though fellowships have divided on the issue, is that all the baptized recognize that in their baptism there is a statement of relationship to the risen Lord.

There is "one God . . . in you all" (v. 6). Paul writing to the Corinthians said, "There be gods many, and lords many" (1 Cor. 8:5). He meant that there is no shortage of gods in the human arsenal but in reality there is one God and those who know Christ know Him. The extent of this knowledge shared by every believer in varying degrees is that He is Father; He reigns above each believer; He works through each believer; He lives in each believer.

The tendency to get off into worship of gods many and lords many does not disappear the moment we come to Christ. Sometimes it intensifies, as the fragmentation and disintegration of so many churches readily demonstrates. But to allow nothing to be God but God, and nothing to be Lord but the Lord, and to recognize Him as reigning over and working through and living in each believer, is the way to unity.

So Paul makes a great appeal to believers to keep the unity that exists and reminds them that it will require considerable effort and assiduous control, much long-suffering and boundless lowliness and meekness. But it is the way to go and it is the way believers must learn to move in their practical Christian experience

Diversity in Community

"But!" (That's a great word in the evangelical vocabulary!) Note that the "but" does not introduce an argument against what has been said, but a fascinating presentation of another aspect of communal Christian experience (see v. 7).

There is a great tendency among those who wish to be together to manipulate the togetherness. So people are encouraged to think alike, then dress alike, then look alike, then sound alike. The result is called unity, but in actual fact is more often a dull uniformity. This is not Paul's idea for the church.

"But," as Paul uses it, introduces the fact that although unity is to be promoted and experienced, diversity is not to be sacrificed. In the midst of the oneness of Christians, there is a diversity that comes from God Himself. He has given various gifts to people. He has made them for different jobs and equipped them for different ministries.

This should come as no surprise to those who know anything of our God. He is a genius at preserving unity in the midst of diversity and protecting diversity in the framework of unity. A few weeks ago I was trying to explain this to some missionaries in Hokkaido, the most northerly island of Japan. We were meeting in a hotel by one of the lakes in an active volcanic area. I asked the people to look out of the window, pointed out that the trees were all green and gave them two minutes to count the shades of green.

They gave up! The green was unified, but the shades were diversified. No green clashed. No greens were ungreen or non-green or part green or anti-green or more green! That's how our God works.

It is in this area that the church has the greatest potential for disaster or for doing something totally different. She can either enforce unity at the expense of diversity by spelling out minute details of belief and behavior, or, at the opposite extreme, she can fall into disarray by allowing total freedom for self-expression of gifts and abilities and life-styles that will make it impossible to detect any community whatsoever. But the real task is to build a community of believers where unity and diversity reflect the work of God like the greens of the forest.

To emphasize his point Paul quoted (rather loosely) part of Psalm 68: "When he ascended up on high, he led captivity captive, and gave gifts to men." Then he explained the way in which the Lord worked. First, He came to earth among the captives and led them captive to Himself. This is an important factor which is sometimes overlooked. The Lord does not come to set us free to do what we like. He frees us by delivering us from one captivity to become captive to Himself.

Then our Saviour ascended into the heavenly spheres of experience, taking all of us who are His captives. There He graciously gave gifts to each of His captives and then distributed the gifted people as gifts to a particular environment. Some commentators see a reference here to the custom of the triumphant Roman emperors who on their return home would throw coins to the rejoicing crowds. So Paul says that Christians are to see themselves as God's gift to a community in the degree in which they live captive to Christ and exercise the gifts given to them by Christ through the Holy Spirit. An exciting and challenging concept!

A healthy church therefore will be one in which there is a growing sense of oneness, which is the result of people eagerly working towards a united life together. It will display a concerted witness to the surrounding society and a many-faceted expression of the ministries for which the Spirit has equipped its people.

Activity in Community

Some gifted people will be more prominent than others in the same way that noses are more prominent than colons. But prominence should never be construed as indispensability, or lack of visibility as unimportance. So Paul says that the more prominent members such as prophets, apostles, evangelists and pastor-teachers (see v. 11) are in the church as Christ's gifts to exercise a ministry that will equip other less prominent members to exercise their ministries. This is a principle of church life that has been sadly overlooked. The objective of all these ministries is to build up the Body of Christ and to bring individual Christians into an increasing maturity that Paul calls "the measure of the stature of the fulness of Christ" (v. 13).

So the two things that should characterize the life of a church living in unity and diversity are *mature individuals* and *mature community life*. The two things should not be confused, because while they are definitely related they are not synonymous. In the athletic world we all know of teams with skilled individual players that are sometimes beaten by teams with less skilled individuals. The reason being that it is one thing to bring an individual to maturity, but an entirely different thing to bring the team to maturity. This requires working on interpersonal relationships, fragile egos, balanced assignments and a thousand and one other things. So it is with the church. And it takes all the gifts to work out all the wrinkles.

It is unfortunate that many churches which "preach the gospel" feel that when they have evangelized people to the point of enabling them to receive Christ they have fulfilled their ministry. On the contrary, their ministry has only begun.

If our world is to see a real picture of what God is doing it needs to see considerably more than individual people finding a panacea for their individual ills. It deserves to be shown a unique society of totally diverse people so united in Christ, that they are working in many ways through their God-given gifts to build up individuals and produce an alternate society that is becoming increasingly mature and attractive. This is the totally different thing that our society needs to see and which our God is committed to show them.

Notes

1. *Theological Dictionary of the New Testament*, Vol. 7, pp. 559,560.
2. Francis Foulkes, *The Epistle of Paul to the Ephesians* Tyndale Bible Commentary (London: Tyndale Press; Grand Rapids: Wm. B. Eerdman's Publishing Co., 1963), p. 112.

8

Born
Again
To
Live
Anew

*Ephesians 4:17-21,14-16,22-32*___

Secular society is the environment in which Christian lives are lived and the church exists. But this secular society needs to be understood for what it is and for what it stands.

Walk Not

Paul is careful to ensure that the Ephesians are clear in their thinking. He holds back nothing in their church's description and insists, among other things, that it suffers from several ills. He compares these ills with the characteristic heathen life which "other Gentiles walk, in the vanity of their mind" (v. 17).

"Having the understanding darkened" (v. 18). This is not to suggest that there is not considerable erudition in the secular world. But when it comes to really understanding the world and man from the perspective of the Creator and Saviour, there is considerable self-induced ignorance and darkness which

is ably encouraged and promoted by the one who blinds men's eyes. The erudition that is void of spiritual insight is one of the most frightening aspects of our contemporary world. Its error spills over into every conceivable area of human existence and endeavor with devastating results.

There is a dynamic in the life of faith that is just not available to those who have been "alienated from the life of God" (v. 18). It ought to be obvious that all other things being equal, the man who has God alive within him has boundless advantages over the one divorced from the life of God. By the same token, the one bereft of divine enabling must be experiencing grave difficulties in functioning as a whole person. The deadness that is the absence of divine life shows itself morally, ethically and spiritually. It leaves people singularly unmotivated in the way they ought to go and perversely motivated towards that which is not to the glory of God or the ultimate well-being of society.

The expression "the blindness of their heart" is translated as "hardness" of heart in the Revised Standard Version (v. 18), the difference being caused by the translator's uncertainty about the origins of the word *porosis*. Some feel it is related to blindness, others to the hardening that takes place in a broken bone when it is being healed. Either way there is no doubt that there is a hardness to things of God even in redeemed people as they relate to everyday living. But the unredeemed demonstrate this much more fully. Some, of course, adopt positions of blatant antagonism; others simply show their hardness by treating the things of God with benign neglect. This attitude permeates personal relationships and societal attitudes and is a powerful force to be reckoned with.

Just a short step from the idea of "hardness" is callousness, which Paul describes as "being past feeling have given themselves over unto lasciviousness, to work all uncleanness" (v. 19). Rejection of moral principle and indifference to moral standards are common attitudes which bring a paralyzing effect to our society and produce all manner of ethical pollution in its fabric.

Paul finishes the statement by including "with greediness." The Greek word for greediness is *pleonexia*, which means literally "to have more." It speaks of the insatiable desire to acquire irrespective of the condition of the one from whom the desired thing is acquired.

Paul is probably referring to desire for all manner of uncleanness. This is particularly relevant to our contemporary society, but it would be a mistake to limit our understanding of greediness to this area of behavior. For ours is a society greedy to have more of everything.

"But," says the apostle, "ye have not so learned Christ" (v. 20). In that terse verse, he reminds the members of the Body of Christ that their life-style is to be in stark contrast to the life-styles of the surrounding society. This difference is to come from the careful appreciation of "the truth [as it] is in Jesus" (v. 21). This truth is to really be heard and learned and the only way that one can be sure that truth has been learned and that Christ is known is by the difference demonstrated in the life of the believer.

Coping with the Cunning

There is another problem confronting the disciple of Jesus and it is the onslaught of various teachings that originate not from God but from "the sleight of men, and cunning craftiness" (v. 14). This leads to the very real possibility of believers being deceived in their understanding and behavior. However, Paul is careful to explain how this can be countered.

Believers are to live in vital touch with the Lord, which is something we all know but don't always know how to accomplish. The explanation the apostle gives appears at first sight to be too complicated to be helpful, but a little study will show in striking fashion how the contact is to be maintained.

Paul uses the analogy of the body once again, showing that Christ is, of course, the Head and that from Him flows all manner of truth and life. But the life and truth that come from Him must flow to various joints that are "fitly joined together" in such a way that "every part" is involved in the "increase of the body" (v. 16). Try to think of energy flowing from a source through various limbs and joints so that every part of the body is receiving the life-giving energy of the source.

The fellowship of believers is the Body. Each member of the Body has a role to play in the transmission of the life of Christ to others so that they will be able to stand out in their contemporary society and also counter the confusions of those who "lie in wait to deceive" (v. 14). But note that every joint is both on the receiving end and the giving end of this life flow. When the head sends the energy to the neck, it is not just for the neck's benefit but also for the shoulder.

But the shoulder must not only concentrate on receiving from the neck but must also be sure to give to the forearm, which in turn passes on what is received to the elbow and so ad infinitum.

It is through the learning of Christ and sharing of the life of Christ through the ministry of believers in the fellowship of Christ that believers function. And to be quite blunt the relative ineffectiveness of many people's spiritual life is easily diagnosed. They are not learning of Him and drawing from Him in the Body.

One fundamental of this *body life*, to use the term popularized by Ray Stedman, is "speaking the truth in love" (v. 15). This means that there is a touch of loving reality about the Body. The members do not show their "love" by avoiding issues that ought to be handled. Neither do they stand firm for "truth" so harshly that they unlovingly destroy those they seek to enlighten. They realistically live together with the well-being of the other person in mind, and do for each other what needs to be done.

From the Old Man to the New Man

Paul further presses home his appeal for a distinctive life-style by reminding them that in their relationship to Christ they repudiated the old life, which he calls the "old man," and gladly accepted the new life or "new man." This position of renunciation and identification is to be constantly borne in mind as they "put off . . . the old man . . . and . . . put on the new" (vv. 22-24).

His description of the old man is far from complimentary as he stresses the intrinsic corruptness and deceitfulness of its nature. This may sound harsh to some ears, particularly if we know unbelievers who demonstrate gracious life-styles and benevolent attitudes. There is no denying the characteristics of such people. But we must not forget that their niceness can be itself deceitfulness in that they themselves feel that by the quality of their lives they will find favor with God. Further we should remember that even the most gracious person has hidden things of the heart that prove the Scripture's evaluation of us all.

The "new man," however, is a creation of God Himself and specializes in "righteousness and true holiness" (v. 24). These qualities are the evidence of the work of God in a life. Righteousness has to do with behavior between man and man. Doing the right thing by people, treating them rightly by God's standards of rightness. The "new man" is therefore deeply committed to social concerns because practical righteousness is an evidence of the work of God in his life.

Holiness is the fulfilling of our obligation to God. It has to do with hidden things of the heart, the aspirations of the soul, the exercise of the spirit in worship. As always Scripture has such a healthy balance which we so often lack. Those who are inclined towards social concern in the Christian community are often suspected of liberalism by those who are inclined to more pietistic aspects of spirituality. And quite naturally the more socially alert members of the Body quite often tend to deride the more "holy" people for their devotional life and concern. But Paul certainly would not be a participant in such a division. He knew that the new man is deeply involved in both righteousness and true holiness.

The new man is to be "put on" while the old man is "put off." Some commentators believe that this has already happened; others see it as something that has to be done continually. There is a sense in which they are both right because believers, by their act of faith in Christ, have both "put off" and "put on." But they of all people know how necessary it is to be constantly discarding, like a filthy garment, the old life and dressing themselves in the regalia of the children of God.

Note the importance of doing both because there will probably be one aspect of this truth that you can do more easily than the other. Some who are particularly introverted can have a great time putting off the old man while those who are more outgoing don't worry themselves too much about that but have a great time putting on something new. My experience shows me that I need to concentrate on the harder part and the other side comes right along! As Simpson asked quaintly, "Who is content with half a pair of scissors?"[1]

The scissors are to be applied in the area of speech. We are to be "putting away lying" (v. 25). Christians lie and sometimes don't seem to be too perturbed about it. They excuse themselves for their lack of truthfulness in many ingenious ways.

Some time ago I heard a young mother testify that she had been an inveterate liar. She had lied to everyone she knew including husband, children and fellow believers. Although she was an active, gifted Christian whose ministry was widely accepted she was not concerned about her lying because she "knew" that God understood. Her twisted logic was that God knew she had a poor self-image and that she needed to hide the truth from people if she was to grow into a more whole person. Fortunately at the time of her testimony she had come to realize that her lying was untenable because it was part of the old man.

"Corrupt communication" is another part of the believer's speech that must suffer some putting off (v. 29). The word used is *sapros* which Thayer translates in his *Lexicon*, "of poor quality, bad, unfit for use, worthless."[2] This certainly enlarges the prohibitions usually placed by believers on their speech habits.

But don't forget that there is to be a putting on as well. Instead of lying we are to speak the truth (see v. 25). It is not enough to abstain from lying without positively engaging in the sharing of that which is necessary for the well-being and edification of the other person, because we are "members one of another" (v. 25). In similar fashion Paul insists our mouths should be releasing "that which is good to the use of edifying" (v. 29). So from a practical standpoint there is no way we can be satisfied with unsatisfactory speech habits or inadequate communication to those who need our ministry of encouragement and "grace."

"Be ye angry, and sin not" (v. 26). Anger comes in various shades and sizes. Some of it is sinful and some of it is righteous. Sometimes it is sinful in the extreme to be angry and other times it is equally sinful not to be angry. The sinful anger is to be put off, the righteous anger is to be put on.

The Lord Jesus knew what it was to be totally frustrated in the obduracy of people and their apparent commitment to thwart the purposes of God. He got angry and yet was without sin. He knew how to "be . . . angry, and sin not" (v. 26). Frustration with awkward people whose tradition, like that of the Pharisees, nullifies the Word of God is not sin. Resentment in the name of God of all that dehumanizes His creation and denies His truth, is anything but sin. This kind of anger needs to be put on.

The other kind of anger needs to be seen as sin and dealt with in summary fashion. In fact it needs to be dealt with on a daily basis: "Let not the sun go down upon your wrath" (v. 26). So when your anger gets the better of you, recognize it is untenable and deal with it before the end of the day by putting on the resources of the new man. This denies you the right of resentment which can lead to all manner of bitterness and estrangement. Christians of all people should be able to handle their tempers aright, particularly in the fellowship of believers.

"Neither give place to the devil" (v. 27). Probably the most fundamental rule of all athletic endeavor is "keep your eye on the ball." Surely the next one is "keep your eye on your opponent." By no means do I wish to suggest that Christianity is on the level of athletic activity. But I do believe that a basic rule often overlooked is what Paul described when he said, "Neither give place to the devil," which is very similar to keeping an eye on your opponent! It means that we should be alert to the fact that careless behavior offers the devil all manner of advantages which he is not slow to take.

So keep your guard up and remember that there is one who is your enemy because you have aligned yourself with his enemy, Jesus Christ. You are a member of a community that he is committed to discredit; so watch him like a hawk. This of course does not mean that you should become paranoid about the devil, because he is a defeated opponent. But even defeated opponents can be dangerous and should be watched very carefully. The worst thing you can do with the devil is disbelieve in his existence. The next is to disregard him. He can still do a lot of damage.

"Let him that stole steal no more" (v. 28). To steal is to deny someone the right to handle responsibly that which is legitimately his. This is an unloving act because it not only robs a person of a possession but, perhaps more importantly, robs him of the opportunity to function in a responsible manner. Accordingly, this unloving, dehumanizing action is totally out of order for the believer and if prior to his commitment to Christ he engaged in such activities in the era of the old man he will desist immediately.

But he must also put on a totally new attitude towards money and the responsible administration of it. He must see work as something intrinsically "good," which is productive in terms of his own being. The money derived from his labor is part of him; therefore, the way he handles his money is an indication of how he sees himself before God. Accordingly, the apostle insists that he should work hard in order "that he may have to give to him that needeth" (v. 28).

Capitalism insists that man should have the right to work and do what he wishes with his earnings. Marxism insists that what he earns belongs to the greater community. The weakness of capitalism is that selfish man is more interested in himself than the greater community and therefore getting money out of him for that community will be harder than pulling teeth. Marxism's weakness is the identical weakness. Selfish man will find all manner of ways of beating the system to protect himself.

So when it comes to money, capitalism and Marxism have some surprising similarities and problems! Christianity on the other hand recognizes the responsibility of the individual to work productively and to share unselfishly. To put on this attitude is one of the greatest evidences of the new man.

"Let all bitterness, and wrath, and anger, and clamor, and evil speaking, be put away from you" (v. 31). As we have already seen, it is extremely easy for believers to become estranged from each other and for all manner of divisions to form as a result. This fragmentation of the Body of believers is as unpleasant and sad as the disintegration of a human body through the ravages of disease. And that is how such things as "bitterness, and wrath, and anger, and clamor, and evil speaking, ... with all malice" (v. 31) should be seen. There has to be the administering of an antidote to such things so that the individual and the Body will not suffer.

But how do we put off such natural tendencies? The answer lies in the other instruction that Paul gives, "grieve not the holy Spirit" (v. 30). We should be aware of the fact that the Holy Spirit who is not an impersonal force, but a divine Person, is grieved by all that the old man does. It is a personal affront to Him and should be seen as such by the believer.

I am fully aware of the fact that we do not usually

personalize the Holy Spirit in this way. We don't really think about Him getting upset but I think, on the authority of the biblical teaching on the Holy Spirit, that we should. If we did begin to look at Him in this light, we would put a much closer guard on our actions. We would spend much less time looking at the justifiable causes of our bitterness and much more time looking at the results of our bitterness on the One whom we profess to love.

It almost goes without saying that the Holy Spirit, when He is called into the picture, is the power through whom we can put off what is to be discarded. He is the enabling One through whom we put on that which is foreign to our nature. The result will be a real obedience to the apostle's injunction, "Be ye kind . . . tenderhearted, forgiving" (v. 32).

Try to imagine for a moment what kind of a community would begin to emerge if individuals began to live together in such a fashion. Then think about the difference that would be demonstrated by this community in the midst of a secular society that is living in such different circumstances. This would be the greatest possible vindication of the gospel of Christ and the most incontrovertible evidence of the reality of Christ being alive and well and actively on the job in our local geographical location.

Notes

1. E.K. Simpson and Frederick F. Bruce, *Commentary on the Epistles to the Ephesians and Colossians* (Grand Rapids: Wm. B. Eerdmans Publishing Co., 1957), p. 105.
2. Joseph H. Thayer, *Greek-English Lexicon of the New Testament* (Grand Rapids: Zondervan Publishing House, 1962), p. 568.

9

Love
Is
Sometimes
Saying
No

Ephesians 5:1-14

A colleague of mine, in a youth center in England, adopted a young Greek boy who had been deaf from birth. He was concerned that the boy should have the best possible treatment and therapy and so my friend brought him to England. On the day of his arrival he sat in on the evening meeting. He could not hear a word and even if he could, he would not have understood. He was doubly handicapped by being deaf in a foreign language!

This however did not stop him functioning, as the speaker of the evening soon discovered to his discomfort. For the boy was a brilliant mimic. He couldn't hear or understand, but he could see and copy. In no time at all he broke up the meeting because he carried on a perfect duplication of all the speaker's mannerisms and characteristics even to the point of drawing attention to his rather large stomach.

Love Mimics

When Paul talked about Christians walking in love,

he gave them the added instruction to do it as follow-ers—"mimics"—of God. In other words, the loving activity of the believer is to be closely related to careful observation of the divine love in action. And the action is to be duplicated in the life of the be-liever. Before we object to this apparently mechanical approach to love, we should note Paul's further quali-fying statement that the mimics should mimic the love of God as those who are God's children and are deeply loved themselves.

When my young Greek friend mimicked he did it for laughs and there was a touch of ridicule in his performance. But there is a kind of mimicry that comes from children, dearly loved by their parents, who want to show their love for their parents by emulating the parents' love. This is the thrust of Paul's statement, "Be ye therefore followers of God, as dear children; and walk in love" (vv. 1,2).

There are two ways in which the love of God is particularly demonstrated to mankind—*giving* and *forgiving.* We are children of God for no other reason than that God chose to give us what we do not de-serve and forgive us for sins that we had committed against Him.

The greatest imaginable illustration of God's loving givingness is the gift of His Son. Christ "hath given himself for us an offering and a sacrifice to God for a sweetsmelling savour" (v. 2). The depth of the giv-ing is seen in the horror of the sacrifice and the im-mensity of the offering. The Sacrifice was acceptable in God's eyes in that it was "a sweetsmelling savour," which is a rather unusual way of saying that it was pleasing and satisfactory to God.

113

The forgiving nature of God is perhaps best illus-trated through checking the full meaning of the word "charizomai." Vine says this means "to bestow a favor unconditionally."[1] The major thrust, therefore, of forgiveness is that it is an act of God stimulated by divine initiative, totally unrelated to the merits or demerits of the recipient. The scope of this forgive-ness is that it reaches people who, like Paul, regard themselves as totally unworthy of such treatment. Its depth and value are measured in terms of the death of Christ being necessary to make it available. For we must always remember that "God for Christ's sake hath forgiven" us (4:32).

Love as a life-style is to be produced in lives that recognize the Father's character and, out of love, wish to emulate this character through mimicking His behavior. If Paul had written about Christian love only in this vein, he would have produced genera-tions of frustrated saints, because there are few more discouraging experiences to be had than trying to emulate the example of an expert when you barely qualify as an amateur.

Because of this, many believers have felt quite jus-tified in overlooking instructions such as this one. But this we may not do because there are many aspects of truth concerning the believer's life of love and they must all be brought into consideration. The Holy Spirit produces love as fruit, but the Lord Jesus com-manded us to love. These are two apparently mutual-ly contradictory statements concerning love, but in actual fact they are mutually complementary. As we obey, He produces. But why should we obey? Be-cause we love the example of our loving Father and the giving attitude of His dear Son so much that we want to emulate the Father and the Son! So all these facets of biblical teaching on love are interrelated and equally important.

How Do I Love Thee?

The subject of love has perhaps produced more statements of poetic majesty than any other subject. Elizabeth Browning's,

How do I love thee? Let me count the ways.
I love thee to the depth and breadth and height
My soul can reach when feeling out of sight
For the ends of Being and ideal Grace,

is a magnificent case in point, particularly if we are poetically inclined. Unfortunately many of us are not. Yet when it comes to love we get poetical and romantic without seeing any necessity for love to get down to where the rubber meets the road.

The Lord Jesus, however, laid the situation clearly before His disciples, "If you love me, keep my commandments" (John 14:15). Nothing very romantic or poetic about that and nothing at all ambiguous about it. Just plain hard-nosed love shown in active response to divine commandments. So the giving and forgiving of God the Father and the Son is to be mimicked by loving children through measurable acts of obedience.

Love is negative. This needs to be stressed because even in the fellowship of believers there is a certain romanticism about love that sometimes appears to be carefully designed to avoid the harsh necessities of dealing lovingly with certain situations. To show how clearly this is expressed by the apostle let me point

115

out to you that his immediate application of the injunction has to do with sexual morality, interpersonal relationships, conversation and matters of belief. Also it should be noted that to Paul, loving meant saying no on occasions. In fact most of his practical instructions at this point are what may be called negative attitudes to the things mentioned above.

This again is something that needs to be re-emphasized in today's confused society because there is a mistaken idea that love is always amenable and in favor of just about anything. In fact there are those who believe that love is the overriding consideration at all times and, provided love is in evidence, anything is permissible even if it is expressly forbidden by God.

Ironically, those who try to apply biblical principles on love are often castigated as being unloving because they do not feel free to override biblical prohibitions in the name of love. After all is said and done, love to God is shown by obeying His commands, not ignoring them or suspending them!

Love and fornication cannot be reconciled. Love was perverted dreadfully in Paul's day, particularly in Ephesus and the surrounding towns that Paul expected to read his letter. There was all manner of "fornication, and all uncleanness" (v. 3).

The Greek word for "fornication" is *porneia* and is obviously related to our familiar word "pornography." If it was necessary for Paul to speak to this subject in his day, how much more in our day when it has been considered necessary to coin new expressions such as "hard-core porn," "soft-core porn" and even "child porn."

It would be a mistake, however, to limit Paul's use of *porneia* to what we today consider pornographic, for there are many people who have no time for pornography who are tremendously enthusiastic about the very thing Paul was forbidding. When he talked of that which was unclean, immoral and covetous, he was thinking of all sexual activity that does not conform to God's clearly enunciated limits. When he talked about sexual perversion, he was not only referring to homosexuality, bestiality, group sex and such like, but also sex before marriage and extramarital sex. In other words, sex outside the God-given confines of marriage was immoral and unclean. The people engaged in these activities were more covetous than loving, whatever they themselves might think.

As a pastor of a large church that touches many areas of city society, I know only too well how relevant this subject is and how desperately necessary. Even believers are falling into the trap of assuming that, because they have warm romantic feelings or hot sexual feelings, God will be pleased with their sexual morality even though it falls into the category of adultery and immorality. Nothing could be further from the truth, and if the churches do not say so, who will?

Strange as it sounds to modern ears, the way to be loving in terms of sexual morality is to say no to sexual commitment outside of marriage, but inside marriage, to gladly say yes as an integral part of the sheer givingness of oneself in every dimension. Sex outside of marriage is basically interested in getting. Otherwise the sexual partners would be giving themselves in the commitment of marriage in sexual abandon. Getting is not a reflection of the character of God, but giving is. So give of yourself in marriage and, as part of the giving, give your body in sexual delight and keep it from another to whom there is no total act of giving. That's more like the love of God.

Having spoken with great force about sexual morality the apostle turns to matters of speech. There is a close connection between the two because Paul sees the way sex figures in our speech as being indicative in our sexual morality. He insists that uncleanness of sexual activity should no more be part of our conversation than our life-style. In the same vein filthiness, foolish talking and jesting should be regarded as "not convenient" (v. 4).

If Paul at this time comes across as a humorless spoilsport, it may be because we do not fully understand what he was saying. By "foolish talking" (*morologia* which is related to "moron") he meant stupid, senseless, dull, nonsensical speech which is a waste of time. "Jesting" (*eutrapelia*) which originally meant quick-witted repartee, later conveyed the idea of witty, dirty talk.

Paul insists that Christian speech should be such that will give thanks to God and edify man. This will demonstrate love for Him and love for fellow humans, but the other kind of speech will do nothing to enhance God in the eyes of man or man in the eyes of his fellow. Therefore the loving thing to do is to be done with this wrong kind of speech.

He further adds the thought of empty ("vain") words being used by people to deceive others and states that this kind of speech brings "the wrath of

God" upon those who listen to it and use it, because they are "children of disobedience" rather than children of God (v. 6). The seriousness of his statement is reinforced by his insistence that such people will not inherit "the kingdom of Christ and of God" (v. 5).

Having shown that the walk of love requires saying no to sexual immorality and verbal looseness, Paul turns his attention to what he calls the "works of darkness" (v. 11). His instructions are not only that Christians should have nothing to do with works of darkness but should "rather reprove them." Here again the loving thing to do is not to mingle freely with those things that oppose God or treat with benign neglect what God forbids.

In our contemporary society the loving thing to do is to demonstrate tolerance to every human action on the assumption that each person has the right to do whatever he wishes. To disagree with this "right" is to adopt a discriminatory attitude; and to take steps to expose their practices as sin is to be a mindless, unloving, hateful bigot. Accordingly, Christians have been very careful about doing what the Bible insists is the loving thing—to boycott and to expose that which is contrary to God's dictates.

Because we have been more influenced by contemporary thought than scriptural principle we should remind ourselves that "the works of darkness," which are so often presented as "works of art," "freedom of expression" or "sexual preferences," are really expressions of alienation from God and willful refusal to accept the truth of God. To see much of our contemporary society in this light, rather than in the light in which it chooses to cast itself, is to recognize the necessity to take a stand on the issues not in the attitude of bigotry but in love for God's principles and concern for man's darkness.

At the time I am writing this book Anita Bryant has taken a public stand based on her understanding of the biblical teaching concerning homosexuality. This has brought much vilification on her head and, sadly, much of it has come from the pulpits of the land. Whatever the outcome of this confrontation, it must be stated loud and clear that Anita Bryant has done what so few believers appear to be ready to do: she has shown her love for God and His principles by taking a stand in His name. She has also shown her concern for those whom she feels are being damaged by a "freedom" that can only lead to destruction, by telling them what they don't want to hear. Whether the methods she has adopted by using the legal processes of the land were the right approach to take, and whether the political affiliations she has made in the process will become counter-productive, only time will show. But these considerations should not be allowed to detract from the courage and conviction she has displayed.

To walk lovingly, then, necessitates saying no to much that our society approves. It requires the courage to be more interested in that which is related to "goodness and righteousness and truth" (v. 9). It demands that our love for God be shown in our insistence on "proving what is acceptable unto the Lord" (v. 10), knowing full well it may not be acceptable to a lot of the people with whom we rub shoulders.

Loving-walking sheds a lot of light on a lot of shady

practice and, as it does, the old command, "Awake thou that sleepest, and arise from the dead, and Christ shall give thee light" (v. 14), is heard again in the society that so often lies in a self-induced stupor. To take the kind of loving position that challenges and rebukes, refutes and exposes is to love in a way that is strange to man but wonderfully familiar to God. But remember, abrasive as this loving is, it never degenerates into a witch hunt and is always aimed at repentance and forgiveness and integration into the light and love of God's relationship with man.

Notes

1. W.E. Vine, *Expository Dictionary of New Testament Words* (Westwood, NJ: Fleming H. Revell Company, 1940), Vol. 2, p. 123.

10

Be Filled With The Spirit And Stay Normal

Ephesians 5:15-20———

Until recent times the Holy Spirit has been conspicuous in His relative obscurity. Sound Christians who rejoice in their trinitarian belief have tended to be strangely quiet about the silent partner in the godhead. In fact it may be fair to say that much evangelical doctrine and practice have so completely ignored the Holy Spirit that it has been more binitarian than trinitarian in character. But all this has been dramatically changed.

Through a variety of circumstances and undeniable happenings the Holy Spirit has made a challenging comeback in evangelical thought and practice. So dramatic has this comeback been that those who have been involved in it have in many instances become so enthralled with the Holy Spirit that they have little interest in the other members of the Trinity.

So we have the strange situation of having trinitarians, on the one hand, functioning to all intents and purposes as binitarians, while others who have "discovered" the Holy Spirit have become pneumatic unitarians. This unsatisfactory state of affairs can be readily rectified if we remember that there are three members of the Trinity, a concept which is hardly the most difficult to grasp but one of the easiest to forget!

Part of the problem has been caused by the fact that some believers, having experienced the Holy Spirit in certain ways, have made this experience an emphasis that is resisted by those who have not had the identical experience. Fortunately the divisions that result are being healed in numerous areas, and the strong unrelenting positions that were first adopted by both sides of the controversy are being considerably modified. What is even more important, the untenable attitudes which had sadly marred the whole situation have been brought more into line with the attitudes that could reasonably be expected from those debating the Holy Spirit, the great unifier of the church.

Drunk and Filled

The straightforward instruction of the apostle recorded in verse 18 has been at the center of the debate concerning the Holy Spirit: "Be not drunk with wine, wherein is excess; but be filled with the Spirit" (v. 18). Exactly what he meant and how the fullness of the Spirit is to be experienced has been variously interpreted and vigorously debated.

First let me point out that there are actually two instructions in the verse. The first one, "be not drunk with wine, wherein is excess" (*asotia* originally

123

meant "incurable" but later became "dissipation or waste"), can be easily overlooked because of the great importance of the second. But it should be pointed out that to the Ephesians, living in pagan Ephesus, drunkenness was a very present problem and probably a vital temptation.

More importantly, I believe that the second instruction can be best understood in terms of the first. Being filled is not unlike being drunk!

There is a school of thought that suggests that to be "filled with the Spirit," it is necessary to be emptied of self. This thinking is understandable because the ministry of the Holy Spirit is often referred to in terms such as "pouring," "rivers of living water," "baptism," "shed forth"—all of which have very definite liquid connotations. But the Holy Spirit is not a liquid. He is a Person. Therefore, we should not make the mistake of thinking of some kind of cathartic experience in which we are emptied of self in order to be filled with Him.

When you understand this, a doorway will open out of despair and discouragement into a more realistic arena of spiritual experience for you.

From a personal viewpoint, the most discouraging times of my Christian experience have been when I was trying to empty myself of myself. I found the experience not unlike trying to get toothpaste back in the tube! Not only because of its impossibility, but also because both the toothpaste and myself had a remarkable facility for squirting out in a new direction just when I thought they were under control.

To be drunk with alcohol it is not necessary for one to be emptied in order to be filled.

Filled "With" or "In"

The expression used by Paul is of great interest and should be studied carefully. There is a significant little word *en* which has caused some headaches over the years. *En* is usually translated "in." Accordingly, some people believe Paul's instruction should read "be filled in spirit," meaning that we should be full-spirited people.

There is a sense in which "be filled in spirit" is a perfectly necessary instruction for believers because the church does not always give the impression of being full of enthusiasts. In fact, Leon Morris in his book, *Spirit of the Living God*, writes about the remarkable inscription on a church bell in Cambridge, "Glory to the church and damnation to enthusiasts."[1] But as Foulkes points out, "To take the expression as meaning merely to be filled in spirit would be to deprive it of the force of meaning that it clearly has in the context, and how can the Christian be filled in spirit but by the Holy Spirit of God?"[2] Accordingly we will take the position that Paul is instructing his friends at Ephesus to make sure that they were being controlled by the Spirit so that their spirits are full.

John Stott in his inimitable, meticulous style has explained in *Baptism and Fullness of the Holy Spirit* that there are four things to note about the verb "filled." "It is in the imperative mood . . . in the plural form . . . in the passive voice . . . in the present tense."[3] If we put all that together we can see that the imperative is a command; the plural is addressed to all those reading the Epistle; the passive means that the filling will be "done to them"; and the present shows that it is to be an ongoing experience. Accordingly, some people like to paraphrase the expression "be being filled with the Spirit."

Captivated, Motivated and Activated

To be drunk with alcohol, one does not have to be emptied in order to be filled; however, one must come under the influence of the alcohol to be controlled by it. So it is with the influence of the Holy Spirit.

I have never been drunk but, as an ex-marine, I have had many opportunities to observe the drunk at painfully close quarters. I have noticed three things about them: they are captivated, motivated and activated by alcohol. I believe, at the simplest level, that is exactly what is involved in being filled with the Spirit.

It is significant that Paul made numerous references to the Holy Spirit in the Epistle before the one we are considering. As we have seen he talked about being "sealed" (1:13), "reconciled" (2:16), "an habitation" (2:22), "strengthened" (3:16), "unity of the Spirit" (4:3); all of which refer to experiences of the Spirit with which the Ephesians were familiar. The Holy Spirit had become the evidence that they belonged to God. He had also become the means whereby God Himself had taken up residence within them. He was the mighty power of the church and the individual believer committed to enabling them to serve God effectively. He was also busy bringing unity and reconciliation in their midst.

Nevertheless Paul was insisting that in addition to all this they should be captivated by Him. It is possible to have an experience of the Holy Spirit without yielding to His control and gladly submitting to His direction. This is brought out most clearly by Paul's heart-stirring instruction, "Grieve not the Holy Spirit of God" (4:30).

Therefore the first thing we should understand about the filling of the Holy Spirit is that once we are sure that He lives within us to be the means of God being seen at work in our lives, we should be prepared to gladly and consistently yield to His promptings and accept His control. There is no filling without a conscious intelligent choice to surrender the will to the revealed will of the Spirit, in the same way that the drunk person surrenders himself to the will of the alcohol.

It is necessary that we be motivated by the Holy Spirit. Alcohol has an effect on its users. Otherwise they wouldn't use it! Some become morose, others giddy. Alcohol makes some people belligerent and others tearful. Some start to sing, others to shout. Drunk people sometimes give their money away, others rob. But one way or another the effect is real and usually discernible.

The motivating presence of the Holy Spirit is no less real and certainly evident. There is, as we have seen, a great motivation to unity when the Holy Spirit is at work in people's lives. This is unquestionably one of the greatest evidences of Spirit-filled living in the community of believers.

Then we should note the great statement "the fruit of the Spirit is in all goodness and righteousness and truth" (5:9). To be primarily concerned with doing what is good and right and true is to give beautiful evidence of the motivating power of the Holy Spirit.

This is particularly the case in a society that appears to be regarding these characteristics as unnecessary relics of outmoded morality. Today it is painfully evident that much motivation is in the direction of that which is popular, comfortable and profitable. None of these motivations is wrong in itself, but when, as so often is the case, there is a conflict between the "fruit of the Spirit" and that which is the contemporary norm, the fruit loses out.

Many a businessman, confronted with a choice between "right" and "profit," will not even think twice before choosing profit. Young persons, when faced with "popularity' and "truth," often will lie rather than risk being ostracized. Not a few women in the subdivision when asked to do "good" have declined because it was not comfortable. So it is relatively simple to see the Spirit-filled person at work because of the sheer contrast of his motivation.

Those under the influence of the Holy Spirit are activated by Him. There has traditionally been something of a tension between those believers who have a concern for the deeper things of the spiritual life and those who are more inclined to such concerns as evangelism and social involvement. Not a few unkind words have been hurled by one opposing party at the other. This is particularly unfortunate, because the differences in outlook would not exist to such a degree if all concerned would take time out to see the biblical perspective.

Our Lord made it quite clear that when His disciples came under the all-empowering might of the Spirit, they would become witnesses starting where they were and reaching to the uttermost parts of the earth. They got the message and were so thoroughly activated by the Spirit's presence that they "filled Jerusalem with [their] doctrine" (see Acts 5:28), became known by some of their enemies as the men who "turned the world upside down" (Acts 17:6), and demonstrated in no uncertain terms that their experience of the Holy Spirit was measurable to a certain extent by the impact they were having in a practical sense on their society. So it was and so it will ever be. The Holy Spirit is not a topic of conversation or debate but the activating force of the Father sent to get things rolling.

Walk Circumspectly

Some years ago I attended a wedding and found myself in an embarrassing predicament. A certain gentleman, who had obviously indulged himself in liquor, came swaying across the room in my general direction. As he drew uncertainly alongside me, he tripped and almost fell. He whirled towards me with as much whirl as he could manage and said thickly, "I know what you're trying to do. You're trying to trip me up." I assured him that I had no such intention and after some attempts at intelligent conversation he decided that the controversy could only be resolved by force! He began to make noble efforts to take off his coat and almost fell on his nose from the effort. Muttering, "I'll teach you to trip me up," he began to adopt a stance which he doubtless thought resembled Joe Louis but in actual fact more resembled an arthritic turtle. Eventually I was able to placate him and he suddenly lost interest in me and staggered away.

I knew he was drunk, not because he was wearing a button in his lapel advertising the fact, but because he was so obviously activated by alcohol. It had affected the way he walked and the way he talked as well as the way he thought. Brain, tongue and feet were all affected by the foreign substance.

Paul expressed with great clarity the fact that similar activities are to be expected in the life of the Spirit-filled person. "See then that ye walk circumspectly" (v. 15).

This fifteenth verse is an obvious reference to the way the Spirit gets into our feet. There is some debate among scholars as to whether the "circumspectly" refers to "see then" or "walk." If it is the former, then the *Revised Standard Version*, "Look carefully then how you walk," is correct. But either way the meaning is quite clear: Great care is to be taken about the life-style of the believer. This is to be reflected by not being "unwise" in our actions but by "redeeming the time, because the days are evil" (v. 16). This means that we should be so ordering our lives that we are buying up the opportunities in the evil days in which we live.

When I was a marine I remember how we were trained to walk with care through minefields and to be most vigilant in dangerous territory so that we could take every opportunity of both defending ourselves and also overcoming the enemy. This is the picture of the Spirit-filled man and his walk. "Look carefully then how you walk."

The brain of the believer is activated by the Spirit so that he is not "foolish, but understand[s] what the will of the Lord is" (v. 17, *RSV*). This apparently simple little statement is full of the most profound teaching. Obviously it presupposes that God has a plan for our lives, but more than that it infers that this plan is knowable.

It is part of the Holy Spirit's ministry to the believer to ensure that he knows what God wants him to know. I have observed that Christians appear to have more difficulty with knowing the mind of the Lord than possibly any other area of their spiritual experience. Aware as I am that there is a number of factors involved I cannot help feeling that the problem may be that the believers who experience the most difficulty have not known the glad revealing and confirming work of the Spirit filling their minds with the knowledge of God's will.

This leads to the very real possibility that their problem of knowing may be related to their unwillingness to do what they already know. They may not be yielding to the Spirit and discovering His infilling.

Then the tongue is certainly affected as Paul shows. He specifies ways in which believers will engage in "speaking . . . singing and making melody" and "giving thanks" (vv. 19,20). He portrays a most attractive picture of believers communicating gladly with each other using all means of corporate and private expression of love and devotion to the Lord. No need for the song leader to think of ways to get the unwilling to sing or the unthankful to express thanks. The Spirit-filled are eager and ready to do both, not only for the benefit of each other but also "to the Lord." I love to think of people singing from the heart to the Lord as they sing with their lips to each other. Then to listen, as they gladly tell with thanksgiving what great things He has done, is an unspeakable joy.

Submitting Yourselves

There remains only one word that I wish to draw to your attention and that word is "submitting" (v. 21). I have no doubt that some of you may have been hoping that I have overlooked it and some of the less charitable may have assumed that I had purposely sidestepped it! No, I've left some of the best wine to the last! I am well aware of the unpopularity of the subject in some quarters and the great emphasis placed upon it in others. It is therefore unfortunate that we cannot look into it at greater length at this point.

All I wish to say is that there should be no difficulty in the life of the Spirit-filled believer on the subject of submitting for one simple reason. The only way they became filled with the Spirit was by being captivated by Him and that is just another way of saying "submit." We will look further into the subject in the next chapter, but I want to conclude by pointing out something that I find most important.

Having talked about the filling of the Spirit, Paul went on to talk about remarkably ordinary matters such as husband-wife relationships, parent-children relationships and employer-employee relationships.

It is an inescapable fact that to Paul the fullness of the Spirit, whatever else it involved, most certainly was to be experienced and demonstrated in the most normal of circumstances and the most mundane environments. This, I feel needs to be stressed because much of the debate on the Holy Spirit has become divorced from the basically down-to-earth fact that it takes the captivating, motivating, activating power of the Holy Spirit to be normal at work, at home and at play.

Notes

1. Leon Morris, *Spirit of the Living God* (Downers Grove: Inter Varsity Press, 1960), p. 90.
2. Francis Foulkes, *The Epistle of Paul to the Ephesians* Tyndale Bible Commentary (London: Tyndale Press; Grand Rapids: Wm. B. Eerdman's Publishing Co., 1963), p. 152.
3. John R. Stott, *Baptism and Fullness of the Holy Spirit* (Downers Grove: Inter-Varsity Press, 1976), p. 60,61.

11

Obey?
Oh
Boy!

Ephesians 5:21—6:9

Recently at a ball game I could not help overhearing the conversation of two young men seated behind me. "Ain't nobody going to tell me what to do!" said one. "Right. Me too! I never take orders from nobody and I never give none to nobody," replied his friend.

I was so appalled by their attitudes that I almost forgot to be appalled by the way they murdered the Queen's English! But, sad to say, their attitude is all too common in our contemporary world. "Authority" has become a dirty word and the thought of submission to authority is abhorrent to many people. This attitude has permeated much Christian living and church experience, as well as family experience and commercial and educational establishments.

When Paul wrote "submitting yourselves one to another in the fear of God" (v. 21), he outlined a principle of major proportions which must be understood and acknowledged particularly in the church of Jesus Christ. The word he used *(hupertasso)* is of military origin and means literally "to rank under." Note carefully that he is not advocating a rigid hierarchical system where people are placed in rank and shown their place in no uncertain terms, but rather that individual Christians should gladly subject themselves to each other. The word used is in the middle voice that, according to the *Theological Dictionary of the New Testament*, "denotes voluntary subordination."[1] Foulkes makes the illuminating comment, "There must be a willingness in the Christian fellowship to serve any, to learn from any, to be corrected by any regardless of age, sex, class, or any other division."[2]

In the Fear of Christ

Obviously the instruction to submit to each other is most unusual. It would presumably be accompanied by unusual explanations and motivational factors if it is to be seriously considered. The unusual factor is provided by the brief but majestic phrase, "in the fear of Christ." The force of this phrase is that the motivation to live a submissive life in the fellowship of believers is not necessarily to be found in the super quality of the fellowship, the infallibility of its leadership and the unbelievable sanctification of its membership, but in obedience to the Lord Jesus.

It is not the irresistible charm of loving people and the unquestioned wisdom and skill of brilliant and godly up front people that stimulates to undying submission and glad sacrificial loving service. It is the Lord who calls us to obey Him and in that obeying tells us to be submissive and sacrificial in attitude in the fellowship of believers. It is our relationship to

Him that motivates to subjection, not the intrinsic worthiness of the one to whom we subject ourselves.

This needs to be understood because so much of the unrest, ill-discipline and selfish individualism in the church is being excused by those who will not submit because they feel that the fellowship is all wrong. They reason that their insubordinate attitude is excusable because of the fellowship's deficiencies.

For the Lord to make such demands of submission on His people may appear at first sight to be unreasonable until we remember that there is order in all areas of God's creation. Dr. Roger Nicole stresses this admirably in his article on "Authority" in the *Baker's Dictionary of Christian Ethics* as follows: "The law is not a tyrannical imposition confining man and cramping his opportunity to enjoy life: on the contrary, it is God's gracious revelation of the structure of the spiritual universe, which teaches man to move along the cosmos lines of force rather than at cross purpose with his true destiny."[3] Man without order can produce only chaos, and chaos leads to pain not pleasure.

To Emulate Christ

Then there is the added incentive to the believer to emulate the example of our Lord Jesus who knew what it was to subject Himself not only to the Father in heaven but also to His parents on earth. There can be no argument in the heart of the enlightened believer about the absolute necessity for a submissive attitude when he considers these facts.

Paul amplified the details of this attitude when he wrote to the Philippians, "Let nothing be done through strife or vainglory; but in lowliness of mind let each esteem other better than themselves" (Phil. 2:3). In this exhortation he was asking the believers in the city of Philippi to be more concerned with the status and condition of their brothers and sisters than with their own. His concern was that they display such a demonstration of the "servant" attitude manifested by our Lord that the fellowship would be one of ministry and concern rather than conflict and selfishness.

Experience the Holy Spirit

The independence demonstrated by so many Christians toward their churches, and their unwillingness to submit to those whom God has set in positions of leadership, is as great a cause for concern as their apparent disregard for the necessity of a humble serving spirit in the community of believers.

This independent unsubmissive attitude is common to our modern society but it does not spring from a modern cause. Paul, writing to the Romans, showed that the "carnal mind" (the natural attitude) was not "subject" to these things and he even went so far as to say it "neither indeed can be" (Rom. 8:7). So the only hope for this working out is through obedient, humble walking in the Spirit. It takes an ongoing experience of the Holy Spirit to make Christians interested in a submissive attitude and an ever-increasing work of grace to see a body of believers begin to move in this direction.

I have spent a disproportionate amount of time on verse 21 for a good reason. Many people have found difficulty with the remaining verses of this chapter because emphasis has been placed on wives, children and employees submitting without a corresponding emphasis on "submission" being something that all believers—whether men or women, parents or children, employers or employees—must do. In the light of verse 21, we must understand that there are times when men must be submissive to their wives and parents to their children and even employers to their employees. If this seems ridiculous to some, let me remind you that Jesus Christ the Lord of glory submitted to a young woman called Mary, according to Luke 2:51! But now it is time to look into the more specific matters of which Paul spoke.

Wives and Submission

Wives are to submit to their own husbands, although we should note that the verb "submit" does not appear in verse 22 in the original. This instruction of Paul has opened him up to considerable vilification on many fronts. But we should not fall into the trap of divorcing verse 22 from verse 21 particularly in the light of the fact that they share the same verb.

Wives are to submit in the context of everybody in the fellowship being voluntarily and mutually submissive! That was what Paul actually said and he should be judged on the whole statement!

There is another factor that should not be overlooked. He added "as unto the Lord" (v. 22). Taken in context, Paul encourages the women to be as submissive as everybody else in the community of believers as they also submit to the lordship of Christ. In addition, they should be submissive to their husbands. There is actually a triple submission: everybody to everybody, each to the Lord, and women to husbands.

I can understand the resentment of many women feeling that Paul told them to submit while everybody else did what they liked. But the Holy Spirit did not inspire Paul to say anything of the sort. He talked about a loving environment where concern and compassion were running wild and in which it would be anything but onerous to be submissive and servant-like, not always looking out for yourself but putting the concerns of others first.

It may be that someone at this point is thinking, "If everybody is submitted to Christ and to each other, why should the wife be given this added instruction?" The answer to that question, I believe, is that the idea of submission incorporates both the connotation of being concerned for the other and also the acknowledging of authority. Therefore, in the family where all should be mutually concerned in serving, it is necessary for there to be final authority and this authority belongs to the husband and should be gladly acknowledged by the wife. It's not unlike a good ball team. If they are going to play well they must have a feeling of mutual respect and be prepared to support each other by covering and playing for each other. But when decisions have to be made not everybody in the team can possibly be expected to make the decision. That's the captain's job and everybody accepts that it is his responsibility. That's how it is in marriage. And when the right relationships exist in a Christian family and towards the Lord there will be little problem when the captain or the man of the house makes the decisions.

In my own experience as a husband and father, I have to say that my wife and children have no doubts that I have the God-given responsibility to make the final decision at times. But I am so aware of my own fallibility that I never make major decisions without adequately exposing myself to the alternatives presented by family in general, and my wife in particular.

Then because someone has to make the final decision in the light of all the input from the family, I carefully do it, but in great humility because I understand the feelings of all concerned. There is no suggestion of authoritarianism or dictatorial attitude on my part. Neither is there a sense of slavery or inferiority on the part of my wife or children, only a great sense of concern for each other and responsibility to God for the decisions made and the actions taken.

In 19 years of marriage I can only remember two occasions when we have had a disagreement which necessitated my putting my manly foot down! My wife says there were three occasions and I was wrong on the first which I have conveniently forgotten and right on the two I remember!

Christ and His Church

To illustrate his point, Paul uses the analogy of the relationship between Christ and the church, finishing up with the words, "As the church is subject to Christ, so let the wives be to their own husbands in everything" (v. 24). The illustration is perfectly clear but the final words "in everything" have posed some problems. There are some who teach that "in everything" means *in every thing*. And, of course, it would appear that they have an undeniable point. However, we should remember that Paul was speaking of an environment of mutual concern and mutual submission. Therefore, some of the problems that have risen in matters of interpretation of this instruction should be seen in this light.

For instance, I have met women who have told me that on the strength of this verse they will do absolutely anything their husbands tell them to do, even to the point of breaking God's law. When I ask them what they would do if their husbands told them to engage in wife swapping, they confidently answer, "We would go along knowing that the Lord would deliver us as He delivered Sarah." But they chose to disbelieve me when I told them that I was aware of situations where women did go along in obedience to their husbands' wishes and, instead of "being delivered," found themselves in the act of adultery.

These women overlook the fact that unsubmissive husbands may make untenable or even immoral demands on submissive wives. The wife must use her God-given capacities to determine in what way she can follow the demands that she submit, not only to her husband, but also to the Lord. The Holy Spirit did not give us a guidebook to be slavishly followed but a living Word to be experienced through the use of all our faculties through the enlightening activity of the Holy Spirit.

Husbands as Servants

The responsibility placed on the husband in this passage is often overlooked and yet, in my opinion, this is one of the most crucial aspects of Paul's teaching. "Husbands, love your wives, even as Christ also loved the church, and gave himself for it" (v. 25). At this point the apostle launched into a beautiful passage on the ministry of Christ to His church and, as is frequently the case, his illustration almost obscured what it was illustrating! In brief, he said that the care of the Lord for His church in sanctifying, cleansing, beautifying, nourishing, and cherishing (see vv. 26-29) was a great mystery but should be real in the relationship existing between man and wife. And it was the husband's responsibility to see that it was done!

This means that the husband will gladly make himself a *servant* of his wife to the extent he can bring enrichment to her in every possible way. This is what Dorothy Pape calls "Revolutionary instructions to husbands" in her helpful book, *In Search of God's Ideal Woman.* [4] How do men make their wives more beautiful? How do they nourish and cherish them? The beauty will come from the contented heart not the corner drugstore. The nourishing and cherishing will come from a stable marriage and a supportive spouse. Incidentally, the word "cherish" means literally "to keep warm" and the word "nourish" is the same word translated "bring them up" in 6:4! So we can readily see that the husband has his hands full when he starts to minister to his wife to make her innerly beautiful, keep her warm, and help her mature!

People often laugh when ministers earnestly expound the theory that Jesus Christ and Christianity have done more to emancipate women than anything

142

else. Pointing to all the submission passages (usually out of context) the critics say with great scorn, "This is the same old stuff the pagans, the ancient Jews, and the Muslims have been teaching for centuries. They all insist that women are second class citizens."

But these people have failed to read the biblical instructions to husbands. Women, according to the Lord and His apostle, are to be treasured as people of infinite value, not chattels of marketable value and pieces of equipment subject to depreciation and trade-in value. It is in this area that women are wonderfully upgraded by Christian teaching and principle. Unfortunately, it is not only the opponents of Scripture who have missed this point but also many of the exponents. They have been so busy putting women in their place that they have missed the beautifully high place God has given them.

But what of the woman while all this nourishing, cherishing and other assorted delights are going on? She will "reverence her husband" (v. 33). The word is literally "fear" but does not include the idea of fearfulness. Rather it means to "revere and respect." The balance of Scripture is once again perfectly clear. Both husband and wife must commit themselves (before the Lord) to serving the other. And neither can go to extremes. Masculine domination is definitely out and militant feminism is out too!

The little woman is not to be treated either as cheap labor or baby doll but as a person who, before God, must be encouraged to the point of maturity and fulfillment.

Husbands must neither rule their roost nor allow themselves to be emasculated, but, through the loving, enthusiastic support of their thoroughly nourished wives, must be whole men living with their families for the Lord.

Children-Parent Relationships

Talking of families, I am reminded it is time to discuss what Paul has to say about parent-child relationships. "Children, obey your parents in the Lord: for this is right" (6:1) and "fathers, provoke not your children to wrath" (v. 4). Immediately, we can see the basic rule of mutual submission being enunciated once again. Because it is "right" and because it is fitting "in the Lord" children are to be obedient as they honor their parents.

But parents must also be careful in the way they exercise their God-given authority. They must avoid driving their kids to distraction by making unrealistic and unreasonable demands. This will require great sensitivity on the part of the parents and loving openness on the part of the children. The kind of openness that one day allowed one of my children to tell me flatly, "Dad, you're prejudiced." And a few weeks later, "Dad, you and Mom have done a great job raising us." This makes it easy for parents to call the shots in love as they bring the kids up healthily and wholly.

Servant-Master Relationships

The same mutuality is seen in the instructions to slave owners and slaves. To our ears this sounds ludicrous but in New Testament times slavery was a political and economic factor that the church could not overthrow. Yet through teaching such as this, the seeds of its eventual destruction were sown. Slaves who treated their masters with respect, working wholeheartedly because they were working "as the servants of Christ, doing the will of God from the heart; with good will" (vv. 6,7), and masters who did "the same things unto them" (v. 9) because they knew they were answerable to the Lord in heaven, produced a slave society totally different from anything the outside world knew.

All Relationships in a Christian Environment

Many people who are having trouble with their own marriages, families and jobs fill the offices of pastors and counselors. We need to remember that Paul in this passage was talking about relationships in a Christian environment. Unfortunately not all people live in such an environment. Therefore, these principles need to be applied with care.

What should wives do whose husbands know nothing and care less for the love of Christ? What is the correct response of children to godless parents in matters where the children have more spiritual insight than their parents? What should modern-day employees do about their relationships to union and management?

All these questions need to be answered, but not from this passage of Scripture alone because it was not designed to be used in such a fashion. But Paul told the Ephesians that, in the environment of church, Christian marriage, family and business, if Christians would become obedient to these principles great would be the transformation in the midst of our sad society. We cannot apply scriptural principles to

Christless situations devoid of the all-enabling Spirit of God, but we can live them in the fellowship of believers and teach them to all who will listen.

Notes

1. *Theological Dictionary of the New Testament*, Vol. 8, p. 42.
2. Francis Foulkes, *The Epistle of Paul to the Ephesians* Tyndale Bible Commentary (London: Tyndale Press; Grand Rapids: Wm. B. Eerdman's Publishing Co., 1963), p. 154.
3. Roger Nicole, "Authority," *Baker's Dictionary of Christian Ethics* (Grand Rapids: Baker Book House, 1973), p. 47.
4. Dorothy Pape, *In Search of God's Ideal Woman* (Downers Grove: Inter-Varsity Press, 1976), p. 291.

12

"Get
Fell
In"

Ephesians 6:10-24

From my experience in the armed forces I have learned that the soldier needs to be thoroughly aware of three things. He needs to know who his enemy is, he must be fully conversant with his own equipment and be clear about his own area of responsibility. Should the occasion ever arise where a soldier in battle cannot identify his enemy, doesn't know how to operate his equipment and has no idea what he is expected to do, it is highly unlikely that he will survive, much less triumph! Unfortunately, this state of affairs is all too common in the community of believers and, accordingly, instead of winning some mighty victories we frequently tend to be on the losing end. So we need to see what Paul had to say about these three things.

Know Your Enemy

There are many pieces of information concerning the enemy to be gleaned from Ephesians 6:10-18. Although Paul does not use the term in this passage, the enemy is generally called *Satan*, which is an Aramaic word for "adversary." He was so called by the Lord Jesus (see Matt. 4:10). Satan is totally opposed to God, God's Son, and God's purposes. As the church is a major part of God's purposes, he is understandably in complete opposition to the church and because believers are the church he is against them too.

So when we talk about Satan the adversary, we mean the one who is totally opposed to us because we are for God. This is a rather frightening prospect and it is interesting to see how believers respond to it. Some become almost obsessed by thoughts of Satan, while others work hard at discounting him and ignoring him as much as possible.

C.S. Lewis in the preface to the *Screwtape Letters* warned that these are "two equal and opposite errors."[1] Satan should be taken seriously because of his immense power, but not too seriously, because he has been defeated and will ultimately perish.

Satan is a slanderer. The word devil *(diabolos)* is derived from the word "to accuse" and this, of course, is one of the devil's major activities. He is apt at accusing God to man, man to God and man to man. His nefarious activities are to be seen in the confusion that has arisen in so many people's minds concerning God.

Even believers at times find themselves prone to doubt God. And when things are hard they are even tempted, like Job, to curse God. Satan is also quick to point out to God the obvious faults of man, as if God is not excruciatingly aware of them. And when it comes to human relationships we can see what a

148

fertile field Satan has in which to operate. All the potential conflicts and misunderstandings are tailor-made for his slanderous accusing activities. No wonder our world lives in spiritual, moral, and societal darkness.

Satan is strong. Paul, as we have already seen was not adverse to mixing his metaphors. So in verse 12 he switched quickly from the picture of a soldier in armor to a wrestler stripped for action. "We wrestle not against flesh and blood" was the expression he used to show how strong is the opponent of God and how great is the conflict in which Christians are engaged.

Those who do believe in Satan often tend to lead such relatively comfortable, uninvolved lives that they don't really believe that he is particularly strong. They know they are expected to believe that he is but they are hard put to think of him other than as a vaguely comic medieval figure. But this is dangerous because to underestimate the power of an opponent is one of the worst mistakes a soldier or a wrestler or a Christian can make!

Satan is subtle. Paul once told the Corinthians, "We are not ignorant of his devices" (2 Cor. 2:11). I have often wondered if Paul was really saying that the Corinthians were fully conversant with the devil's tactics. If they were conversant they were certainly not using the intelligence they should have gained about his tactics very well. The same is true of our contemporary church. The devil does have his "wiles" (the Greek word is *methodia*, which is quite illuminating!) which haven't changed much since Eden. Of course, he hasn't needed to change them because he's been doing well with them from that time on. But he is subtle and skilled and organized, and we should not forget it.

Satan is structured. Foulkes with delightful understatement says, "The thought of a personal devil, though found in every part of the New Testament, does not commend itself to all quarters today. Still less does the idea of the 'principalities' and 'power' of evil and spiritual 'rulers of the darkness of this world.' "[2]

The structure of devilish activity of which Paul speaks is hard for us to understand. What exactly he meant in all its detail has been the subject of considerable debate. But there are two things that are clear: first, these structured forces of evil that oppose the Lord (under the devil's direction) are to be found operating in many areas of the world's system; secondly, as Paul pointed out in the first chapter, when Christ rose from the dead and ascended to the Father, all these forces were included in the "all things" which were put under His feet.

So once again we see the correct perspective. The satanic forces are big but God is much bigger. They can more than match us but our Lord is more than a match for them—and we are in Him!

Satan is sinful. Paul calls the devil "the wicked" one (v. 16). This means that he is rotten through and through. He was, of course, made by God so his intelligence and attributes were beautiful and superb in their original condition. Even now, in his totally abused state, Satan shows something of the wonder and majesty of God in his range and capability. But the devil uses his attributes only for evil because he is interested only in evil. His methods are dirty, his motives are reprehensible. He has no moral integrity and will adapt anything to suit his purposes and use anybody to further his ends. His scruples are nonexistent. He is unmoved by pain and unconcerned by anguish. He feeds on famine and builds on destruction. He is filthy in his intent and formidable in his ability.

Satan is spiritual. Paul told us in the early part of the Epistle that we reside in the spiritual realm now that we are "in Christ." What he did not say at that time was that the devil also operates in the spiritual realm. So contrary to what many believers have been led to believe, Christianity is not just "Jesus and me on the Jericho road," but me in Christ in the area where Satan does his work.

Satan specializes in touching the human spirit and challenging the rights of Christ to this part of man. He is in vicious conflict with the risen Lord over the souls of men, both before they come to Christ and after they are found in Him.

So every person who moves into experiences of a spiritual nature should be thoroughly aware that he is moving into areas of bad spiritual forces as well as good. This is why there are so many spiritual counterfeits. The one who operates in the same "heavenly places" (v. 12, *RSV*) where we are seated in Christ, knows that before we come to Christ he has us blinded. But once our eyes are open to spiritual reality Satan can't close them again. But he can do a great job of confusing us!

A surgeon friend told me a few days ago that marvelous as the human eye certainly is, he is much more thrilled with light. For as he pointed out, even an open eye can't function without light. In fact, without light this most magnificent piece of bodily equipment is practically useless. The opening of spiritual eyes to the light in Christ is great but the clouding of that light by the Lord's opponent can do awful harm. And, unless Satan is countered, even your open eyes see nothing much at all.

Know Your Equipment

Sorry to keep talking about the marines but my time served had no greater benefit for me than providing illustrations! So I have to use them to justify all the blood, sweat, and tears! One of the things we had to learn was the use and operation of our equipment. In fact, the weapons we were taught to use had to become such an integral part of our lives that we needed to know how to dismantle, clean and re-assemble them in total darkness. Working on Murphy's Law, which states that if anything can go wrong it will and that if it goes wrong it will go wrong at the worst possible time, the military authorities know it is so important that soldiers understand their equipment.

Paul felt much the same about the "armour of God," which he told the believers to "take" and "put on" (vv. 11-13). The word "whole" does not appear in the original but is necessary to translate the word *panoplia* which means the complete equipment of a heavily-armed Roman soldier. Note that it is the "armour of God" and this can mean the armor that God "wears" or "provides."

Isaiah said of Jehovah, "For he put on righteous-

152

ness as a breastplate, and a helmet of salvation upon his head" (Isa. 59:17) and there is an obvious link with Paul's illustration. Therefore, we may see something of that which the Lord puts on in His character and which He provides for us so that we may be identified with Him in the conflict.

The equipment has to be "put on." There has to be a definite action on the part of the believer in carefully dressing for battle. To look at the armor won't do.

The basic piece of a soldier's equipment is the belt. So, the first action is to ensure that the "loins [are] girt about with truth" (v. 14). If the belt is too loose his equipment, which is fastened to it, will impede his movements. So belts are important. The Christian has to ensure that there is truth, reality, integrity at the very base of his profession. Without this there is only disaster for all concerned. To be found in battle with someone who is not real and reliable is to encounter terrible danger. To try to match wits and muscle against the forces of evil with "soldiers" who are not real is to invite total defeat. What a word to the church of today!

Having checked out his belt, the soldier then carefully buckles on his breastplate. The breastplate, of course, protects his heart. Paul sees the "breastplate of righteousness" as an integral part of the believer's equipment.

The term righteousness can be understood in two different ways. Simpson identified the problem of interpretation as follows, "Here again is the appellation objective or subjective? Are we to understand imputed or, inwrought righteousness thereby?"[3] He adds that most commentators give their vote to the latter and it would seem to me that while the former is included in the latter, the apostle was probably saying that the soldier must guard his heart by a consistent life, a practical right living. Otherwise he won't last long in the battle.

I learned the hard way that boots are as important to a soldier as belts. Not that I personally had trouble but some of my friends did. In fact, on one occasion my buddy had such badly blistered feet that I had to carry him and his equipment on top of all my equipment. I was not fit for very much after that experience!

Care must be taken to see, as Paul says, that feet are "shod with the preparation of the gospel of peace" (v. 15). The word "preparation" probably refers to a "prepared foundation" upon which the soldier can stand. This foundation is the good news that brings peace so that even in the thickest battle he has the firm conviction that he is fighting in the name of Christ for the truth, and this brings peace. Without this conviction his usefulness will be suspect.

A soldier in Paul's day used a shield. Paul's reference to the "fiery darts" may relate to a military practice of firing flaming arrows into defensive positions. This certainly is a dramatic picture of the burning temptations that constantly plague the Christian. Burning lust, blazing temper, and fiery trials are the common experience of those who would live rightly before God in the secular scene.

But Paul prescribes the God-given defense. It is the "shield of faith" (v. 16). This piece of equipment was a large heavy shield behind which the beleagured soldier could take refuge. Paul makes no apology for telling the Ephesians that it will be necessary for them to hide themselves in Christ through complete faith and dependence. This may not sound very soldierly, but even the best soldiers have to admit with Shakespeare that occasionally "the better part of valour is discretion." Only the foolish Christian tries to tackle his enemy without recognizing his utter dependence upon the Lord.

A soldier is not equipped for battle without a helmet. Some soldiers who are physically fit and well-equipped become incapacitated for all practical purposes. Their minds fall apart. Shell shock, battle fatigue are some of the names for this strange affliction. But the Christian soldier need never lose his mind for he has protected it by taking the "helmet of salvation" (v. 17). Salvation refers to much more than initial deliverance from the penalty of sin. In this instance, salvation probably refers to the ongoing deliverance from sin's power that God promises to those who trust and obey. With this constantly in mind, the soldier can and must be strong even though he faces tremendous odds.

This concludes the armor except for one item. But what an item! So far the armor has been designed purely for defense, but the soldier of Christ is called to take the offensive weapon.

A soldier needs "the sword of the Spirit, which is the word of God" (v. 17). The Lord Himself gave the perfect demonstration of the use of this weapon in His encounter in the wilderness. When the devil tempted Him through partial representation of the truth, the Lord knew the Word well enough not only to recognize the perversion of it but also to be able to counter with the truth of it. This is sword-handling of the greatest skill.

There is great need for believers who will take the time to develop skills in the Word of God and who will then use the Bible as a weapon against error and as a means of communicating truth. There are no shortcuts to this efficiency and effectiveness so the sooner our churches and schools start to turn out more people equipped in the Word, the sooner we can expect more victories in the realm of spiritual warfare. Many of our contemporary methods of engaging the devil in conflict are devoid of spiritual cutting power because they leave out the "sword of the Spirit." The alternate equipment being proposed by many is about as suitable and effective as an issue of water pistols to halt the advance of a panzer division.

Know Your Engagement

Those of you who have been in action know how important it is that each man should know what is expected of him. There are four things Paul says the believer should do.

First, the believer should "be strong" (v. 10). Literally the instruction is "be strengthened" which makes a lot more sense. It's no good telling someone weak to be strong. But you can certainly tell him to allow the strengthening process to take place in him, particularly if he knows about the strength which is his "in the Lord" and "in the power of his might."

Second, the believer should stand, "having done all, to stand" (v. 13). This means that it is necessary to take a definite position against the attacks of the devil and not to concede an inch. Even in the heat of the battle, the believer should be firm and when the dust has settled and the smoke has cleared he should still be standing.

Third, the disciple of Christ should "withstand" (v. 13). This is quite different from "standing." When Paul was concerned about Peter's ambivalence in the matter of Gentile converts adhering to Jewish practices, Paul "withstood him to [his] face" (Gal. 2:11). This, of course, shows that there is a place for the believer to adopt an aggressive stance and take the fight to the strongholds of Satan as Paul did to Peter. This we expect missionaries to do in far-off lands, but the strongholds are waiting to be stormed in every land and this is part of the engagement.

Finally, the believer should be "praying always with all prayer and supplication in the Spirit" (v. 18). There is no need at this point for us to talk much more about prayer because we have studied the prayers of the apostle contained in this Epistle. All we need to note is that even though he was an "expert prayer" himself, he needed all the prayer he could get for the work of the Lord in general and himself in particular. A salutary reminder that part of our job in the spiritual conflict is to be in earnest about prayer!

So there we have it. And I know of no better way to conclude this chapter and the study of the whole Epistle than to quote Charles Wesley's great hymn:

Soldiers of Christ arise,
And put your armor on,
Strong in the strength which God supplies
Through His eternal Son;

Strong in the Lord of hosts,
And in His mighty power,
Who in the strength of Jesus trusts
Is more than conqueror.

Notes

1. C.S. Lewis, *The Screwtape Letters* (Macmillan Publishing Company, Inc., 1961).
2. Francis Foulkes, *The Epistle of Paul to the Ephesians* Tyndale Bible Commentary (London: Tyndale Press; Grand Rapids: Wm. B. Eerdman's Publishing Co., 1963), p. 172.
3. E.K. Simpson and Frederick F. Bruce, *Commentary on the Epistles to the Ephesians and Colossians* (Grand Rapids: Wm. B. Eerdmans Publishing Co., 1957), p. 147.

Bibliography

Baxter, J. Sidlow. *Explore the Book*. Grand Rapids: Zondervan Publishing House, 1951.

Davidson, Professor F. *The New Bible Commentary*. Grand Rapids: Wm. B. Eerdmans Publishing Co., 1953.

Exell, Joseph S. *The Biblical Illustrator*. Grand Rapids: Baker Book House, 1973.

Foulkes, Francis. *The Epistle of Paul to the Ephesians*, Tyndale Bible Commentary (London: Tyndale Press; Grand Rapids: Wm. B. Eerdman's Publishing Co., 1963).

Henry, Carl F., ed. *Baker's Dictionary of Christian Ethics*. Grand Rapids: Baker Book House, 1973.

Lewis, C.S. *The Screwtape Letters*. New York: Macmillan Publishing Company, Inc., 1961.

Morris, Leon. *Spirit of the Living God*. Downers Grove: Inter-Varsity Press, 1960.

Moule, H.C.G. *Ephesian Studies*. London: Hodder and Stoughton, 1900.

Pape, Dorothy. *In Search of God's Ideal Woman.* Downers Grove: Inter-Varsity Press, 1976.

Simpson, E.K. and Bruce, Frederick F. *Epistles to the Ephesians and Colossians.* New International Commentary on the New Testament. Grand Rapids: Wm. B. Eerdmans Publishing Co., 1957.

Stedman, Ray. C. *Riches in Christ.* Dallas: Word, Inc., 1976.

Stott, John R. *Baptism and Fullness of the Holy Spirit.* Downers Grove: Inter-Varsity Press, 1964.

Thayer, Joseph H. *Greek-English Lexicon of the New Testament.* Grand Rapids: Zondervan Publishing House, 1956.

Vine, William E. *Expository Dictionary of New Testament Words.* Old Tappan, NJ: Fleming H. Revell